THE WRIGHT STYLE

THE INTERIORS OF FRANK LLOYD WRIGHT

CARLA LIND

Thames & Hudson

First published in the United Kingdom in 1992 by
Thames & Hudson Ltd
181A High Holborn
London WC1V 7QX

www.thamesandhudson.com

First published in paperback in 2004

British Library Cataloguing-in-Publication Data
A catalogue record for this book is available from the British Library

ISBN 0-500-28527-6

Printed and bound in Singapore

Quotation sources: page 20. *House Beautiful,* November 1955. Hearst Corporation. page 23. *Frank Lloyd Wright: His Living Voice.* The Press at California State University. © 1987 Frank Lloyd Wright Foundation. pages 28–31. *In the Cause of Architecture: Frank Lloyd Wright.* An Architectural Record Book. © 1975 McGraw-Hill, Inc. page 64. *An Autobiography.* Frank Lloyd Wright. Duell, Sloan and Pearce, 1943. © 1932, 1943, 1977 Frank Lloyd Wright Foundation. page 99. *Frank Lloyd Wright's Fallingwater: The House and Its History.* Donald Hoffmann. © 1978 Dover Publications, Inc. pages 113, 120. *The Pope-Leighey House.* Terry B. Morton, ed. National Trust for Historic Preservation, 1969. page 165. *R. M. Schindler House, 1921–1922.* Produced for Friends of the Schindler House. Perpetua Press. ©1987 Kathryn Smith.

Photograph, page 1: The entrance gate Frank Lloyd Wright designed for the Lovness studio in Stillwater, Minnesota, picks up geometric designs in the house itself. Wright's favorite color, Cherokee red, was chosen for the gate's iron pipe. [Domino's Center for Architecture and Design]

Photograph, pages 4–5: Wright's organic architecture seamlessly blended outside and in, carefully framing views of nature. The living room window of his home Taliesin captures his beloved Wisconsin countryside. An art glass design from the Heath house in Buffalo, New York, is set into the window. [© Yukio Futagawa]

Photograph, pages 2–3: Fallingwater, Wright's famous house cantilevered over a waterfall, melds house and site like few other buildings have ever done. The stone and concrete masterpiece rises from the rocky bed of a mountain stream near Mill Run, Pennsylvania, and is embraced by abundant vegetation on the hillside. [Christopher Little]

Photograph, pages 6–7: The barrel-vaulted children's playroom in Wright's own Oak Park home shows how the young architect was able to expand space visually even early in his career. The pureness of the geometric forms and the decorative elements in the room reflect Wright's training with Froebel blocks when he was a boy. [Jon Miller, © Hedrich-Blessing]

Produced by Archetype Press, Inc.

Project Director: Diane Maddex
Designer: Robert L. Wiser
Catalogue Research Assistant:
Alison Maddex

Inside cover design by Robert L. Wiser. Courtesy Schumacher.

Opposite: Wright's Dana-Thomas house in Springfield, Illinois, completed in 1904, is a symphony of autumn colors, geometric designs, and dramatic spaces. The magical art glass window patterns are derived from natural forms, most notably the angular shapes of sumac leaves. [© Judith Bromley]

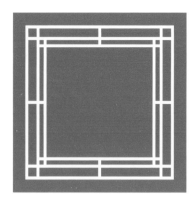

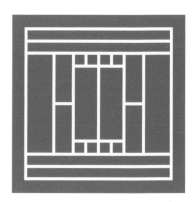

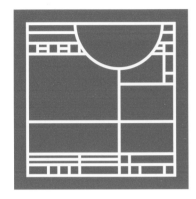

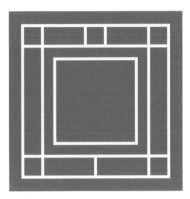

INTRODUCTION

Frank Lloyd Wright was America's very own architect. He was a product of the country's pioneer, can-do spirit who revolutionized the way Americans thought about their buildings and towns. Drawing inspiration from his native midwestern prairie, he coaxed Americans out of their boxlike houses and into wide-open living spaces that suited the American lifestyle. He rejected the classical designs borrowed from other worlds that so dominated the architecture of the late nineteenth and early twentieth centuries. Instead, he gave America a blueprint for its own architecture, one based on simplicity and the lessons of nature. He called it organic architecture.

His career spanned seven decades and two centuries. From 1885 until his death in 1959, he received more than a thousand commissions, nearly half of which resulted in completed structures. Six out of every seven of these still stand. Wright remains the most prolific architect America has ever known. His buildings are scattered from coast to coast, in thirty-six states and three foreign countries. Nestled into woods, projecting from mountaintops, stretched over suburban acres, sculpted from hillsides, defining city blocks, or blending with the desert floor, nearly every building is a unique response to the client and the site for which it was designed. Equally diverse are their functions. The versatility of Wright's talent resulted in masterpieces for living, working, worshiping, learning, performing, and even a plan for an entire city. Their beauty stems from the essence, the very nature, of each individual project. The architecture was not imposed on the building's purpose but was a response to it.

Wright's greatest contribution was his fresh look at residential architecture, the focus of this book. Throughout his career, he was obsessed with defining the perfect living space for contemporary life. In fact, an overwhelming majority of his commissions—eighty percent of his more than four hundred surviving buildings—are residences or their outbuildings. He carefully studied society, its innovations, its absurdities, and its relationship with the natural world. He saw an America that was informal, independent, asymmetrical. Yet it was housed in confined, formal, symmetrical boxes that were adorned with elements drawn from European history. He sought to give America its own architectural identity that fit its people, landscapes, and technologies. And what an impact he had.

Wright's ideas have so permeated our architectural world that we have lost track of the source. His open floor plans led to

family rooms, kitchens open to living areas, indoor spaces open to outdoor living spaces, garden rooms, decks, and carports. His use of glass opened window walls and brought generous amounts of light and inspiring vistas into rooms. He altered America's collective subconscious. By bringing together many elements and inspirations, most neither new nor original, he was able to synthesize fresh new forms that reflected the character of the nation.

His productivity appears even greater when each commission is analyzed. Every one of the more than three hundred residences he designed was a complex composition of numerous interrelated elements. He created not merely the shell of a building but its decorative arts as well. The art glass windows and skylights, furniture, light fixtures, textiles, carpets, fireplace andirons, wall murals, wall finishes, any integral ornament, and landscaping all were part of the unified design he envisioned for a client. This approach resulted in thousands of individual designs. Fortunately, he was always surrounded by devoted apprentices and artisans who could interpret and execute his design ideology in its many manifestations. Although he tried, it was humanly impossible for one person to follow through on each detail of every job. By necessity, his apprentices became ambassadors—extra hands—enabling Wright's genius to have an even deeper and broader impact.

Wright's need to communicate his revolutionary vision was insatiable. But so is the public's hunger for his ideas. Those who came in contact with him, whether in an audience, on a street, or in his office, were left with an indelible memory that they would speak of for years to come. Periodic surveys still rate him as America's greatest architect, despite the fact that he has been dead for more than thirty years.

His words, as well as the beauty of his designs, have gradually sensitized more and more American families so that when they look for a home or discuss plans with an architect, they have the courage to express what they want and need, expecting a sensitive, meaningful response. He brought architecture to the people. Wright made us feel that good residential architecture was within our reach.

Contrasts that appealed to Wright can be seen at Fallingwater, where at night light plays against dark, glass against stone, horizontal against vertical, elegance against simplicity. [Christopher Little]

THE WRIGHT STYLE

FRANK LLOYD WRIGHT'S ARCHITECTURE WAS ROOTED IN NATURE; HE CALLED IT ORGANIC. AT THE HEART OF HIS WORK WAS SIMPLICITY, HARMONY, UNITY, AND INTEGRITY. HE TOSSED OUT OUR BOXLIKE SPACES, FOREVER CHANGING THE IDEA OF WHAT A HOUSE COULD BE.

Previous pages: Nature was Wright's greatest teacher. His lessons were rooted in the essence of natural forms, rhythms, colors, and structures. The roots of a tree, the palette of the season, and the filtered light of Wisconsin woods became an inspirational textbook for his organic designs. [Michael J. Shedlock]

Opposite: The dining room Wright created for his Oak Park home in 1895 exemplifies the unity he achieved even in his earliest work. He reached beyond the design of the house itself to all of the elements in the room. Wright took control of the entire space by designing the furniture, including the high chair; the recessed lighting, which was filtered through a wooden grille; and the cabinets, crafted to conceal the radiators. The result was a total, unified environment, one of the first of many he strove to create in his seventy-year career. [Jon Miller, © Hedrich-Blessing]

ORIGINS

There is a certain irony in talking about a "Wright style," because the uniformity this term implies probably would be viewed negatively by Wright himself. To Wright, the inherent differences in each building, designed to fit the needs of each client and the attributes of each site, defied grouping it into a category. The only "style" involved was how well a building was designed to serve its own purpose. Wright suggested that "as humanity develops, there will be less recourse to the 'styles' and more style . . . that quality in each that was once painfully achieved by the whole." His own work clearly reflected this attitude. Each Wright-designed structure was unique and vital. That was *his* style. Yet there is an undeniable commonality about the vast number of designs that burst forth from this artistic genius.

Frank Lloyd Wright's creations were based on a life philosophy that was undeniably rooted in his childhood. Further shaped by his life experiences, his designs developed distinct attributes that, when repeated, pushed some of his buildings helplessly into sub-styles such as Prairie (1901–1913), textile block (1917–1924), and Usonian (1936–1959), terms used by Wright himself. While useful, these terms do not do justice to the individuality of each building, and they do not describe many of his designs that cannot be neatly labeled. Like any great artist, his work has been grouped into periods to denote shifts in his personal and professional direction. Such categories, like his buildings, are not boxes; instead, they are open and informal shelters. Wright called the totality of his work organic architecture. This concept provides the breadth and flexibility required to define Wright's style as he and his followers have practiced it for the past century. It is far more enduring than the term "style" implies.

To Wright, standardization was useful but should not limit the architect's vision. In fact, his fascination with technology and his desire to bring good design into the homes of average Americans led to several production-line projects, for prefabricated houses, glassware, fabrics, wallpapers, and furniture. By agreeing to design lines of interior furnishings, he was certainly selling his "style," because for the most part they would not be used in buildings he designed.

Many fibers in Wright's life were woven together to create a unified, ideological tapestry just as all of the elements in his buildings were combined and interrelated to yield a complete composition for living. Wright acknowledged that some of the fibers contributed more to the ultimate fabric than others.

UNITY

The origins of Frank Lloyd Wright's aesthetic sensibility can be traced to his youth. His mother, Anna Lloyd Wright, the child of tough, Unitarian, Welsh farmers, introduced her son to many of the experiences that shaped his life. Anna Lloyd-Jones was raised in the Wisconsin River Valley near Spring Green, Wisconsin, and she loved the earth. Wright described her as being "in league with the stones of the field." Anna had a vision for her son—that he would become a great architect. Thus, his early education, at home and at school, was directed toward this goal. She provided a simple but stimulating environment for his learning. Her maternal influence was augmented by the dominating Lloyd-Jones family. Wright frequently visited the Wisconsin farms of his uncles and learned firsthand about hard work, simplicity, and self-confidence.

The concept of unity was a compelling early lesson. So intrinsic was it to the Unitarianism of his family that it must have played an indelible role in creating his world view. As he recalled in his autobiography, "Unity was their watchword, the sign and symbol that thrilled them, the Unity of all things!" Wright's grandfather, father, and uncles were powerful preachers who pounded the concepts of their faith into the depths of the soul of the child. Unity—a oneness with the world, with God, with all forms of life. Truth, truth above all, truth against the world, the beauty of truth. This refrain also echoed in Wright's young world. How could these concepts be forgotten as he forged his own philosophy? They could not. They became its foundation.

Left: Wright felt especially at home in the Wisconsin countryside. Here he surveys the view outside Taliesin about 1928. [Frank Lloyd Wright Archives]

Opposite above: The Wrights enjoyed an active family life. Just a year after their marriage in 1889, Wright (seated at right) and his relatives gathered on the front steps of his Oak Park home. With him, from left, are Jenkin Lloyd-Jones, an uncle; Susan Lloyd-Jones, an aunt; his sister Jane; his wife, Catherine, with baby Lloyd; Anna Lloyd Wright, his mother; Maginel, a sister; and Mary, a cousin. [Frank Lloyd Wright Home and Studio Foundation]

Opposite bottom: Wright also found quiet moments to read and take this self-portrait on the terrace in Oak Park. He saw his home as a refuge and a stimulating gathering place. [Frank Lloyd Wright Archives]

MUSIC

Wright's father made a lasting impact on the architect's aesthetics, although some historians have considered him, unlike Wright's mother, an insignificant and somewhat temporary influence. Like the Lloyd-Jones family, William Russell Cary Wright also was a Unitarian, a minister as well as a lawyer and musician. From him, Wright discovered his passion for Baroque music. As a child, he would lay awake listening to his father playing Beethoven on the piano. The interplay of the notes, the minor themes and major themes, the harmony, the building, the movement from general to particulars, all deeply affected the way he viewed his world. Music did not merely entertain him but also enriched his life in many ways. It provided an analogous system that he could use to help translate his ideas into another art form, architecture. In his autobiography, Wright described the commonalities between an architect and a musician: "the striving for entity, oneness in diversity, depth in design, repose in the final expression of the whole. I am going to a delightful inspiring school when I listen to Beethoven's music."

In a special edition of *House Beautiful* magazine published in 1955, Wright, then eighty-eight, wrote:

What I call integral ornament is founded upon the same organic simplicities as Beethoven's Fifth Symphony, that amazing revolution in tumult and splendor of sound built upon four tones, based upon a rhythm a child could play on the piano with one finger. Supreme imagination reared the four repeated tones, simple rhythms, into a great symphonic poem that is probably the noblest thought-built edifice in our world. And architecture is like music in this capacity for the symphony.

To Wright, both music and architecture were sublimated mathematics. He credited his father with making the comparison by referring to a symphony as an "edifice of sound."

Music was always an integral part of Wright's life at Taliesin. When he was there he made time to play the piano, a skill his father taught him at an early age. Music gave Wright relaxation and inspiration. In the masterworks of Bach and Beethoven he found analogies to architecture. [Ezra Stoller, © Esto]

Right: Nature inspired Wright in many ways. Concrete sprites at Taliesin West recall the patterns of desert cactus. [Richard Bowditch]

Below: Limestone outcroppings were translated into naturally laid stone walls at Taliesin. [Balthazar Korab] Yucca flowers, in the hands of Wright student Gene Masselink, became an abstract geometric pattern. [Tony Puttnam, Frank Lloyd Wright Foundation]

Opposite: Wright borrowed the angular forms of mountains for the rubble walls of Taliesin West. A sumac plant was abstracted to create art glass for the Dana-Thomas house. [Tony Puttnam, Frank Lloyd Wright Foundation]

NATURE

Nature, above all else, was Wright's most inspirational force. He advised his students to "study nature, love nature, stay close to nature. It will never fail you." His childhood experiences on the family homesteads in the rugged, driftless area of southwestern Wisconsin put him in touch with the rhythms, patterns, colors, and systems of nature. The simple concept of the interdependence of all living things was absorbed at an early age. Nature was synonymous with God to Wright, and it was his greatest teacher. Through his mother, Wright also learned to appreciate the work of the naturalist writers of the time: Whittier, Lowell, Emerson, Blake, and Thoreau. Their writings encouraged him to find wisdom in the natural world.

In 1953, in one of his Sunday morning spontaneous talks to his students, Wright advised them:

The place for an architect to study construction first of all, before he gets into the theory of the various formulas that exist in connection with steel beams, girders, and reinforced concrete, is the study of Nature. In Nature you will find everything exemplified, from the blade of grass to the tree, from the tree to the geological formations to the procession of the eras beginning with the first from the sea downwards. . . .

That doesn't mean you are to go out and just look at the hills and the ways the animals conduct themselves. . . . The study of Nature, Nature with a capital N, Nature, inner Nature, Nature of the hand, of this apparatus, of this glass. The truth concerning all those things is architectural study.

He did not suggest copying nature but, instead, allowing it to be an inspiration, understanding the fundamental principles and elements—its essence. The visual delights that nature provides became a part of his designs as well. The sympathetic relationship between site and building, the easy transitions from the inside to the outside, the gardens and planters all illustrate a respect for the natural world that is compelling. It is difficult to visit one of Wright's buildings and not interact, in a memorable way, with its setting. He built homes around trees, rather than remove them. He used the sun's power to help warm the rooms and provide an ever-changing pattern of light and shadow. He framed views, both nearby and distant. He borrowed nature's devices to provide repose using the line of the horizon, to extend reach using the cantilever like a branch, to create protective shelter like a natural cave. The interplay of people, building, and site was harmonious and masterful.

GEOMETRY

As a result of Anna Lloyd Wright's continuous search for educational techniques that would encourage young Frank's creative skills, she discovered the Froebel blocks. These teaching tools for Friedrich Froebel's kindergarten education program introduced Wright to geometry, spatial relationships, and systems in a fundamental way. The program's basic theme was that child's play could be gently guided, using specific techniques, toward a greater appreciation for the elements and laws of nature. The tools were simple, pure shapes, unlike the gawdy, frivolous toys of the period.

It is from the Froebel "gifts," as they were called, that he learned the basic forms of nature—geometric forms—in two and three dimensions. First, he worked with colored yarn shapes, then smooth maple blocks in cubes, spheres, and triangles, then colorful cardboard shapes made into patterns on a tabletop grid. Each exercise was a new problem that challenged the budding designer. As a child, he spent hours with these gifts, later attributing to them a formative and lasting influence on his architecture. Their impact was apparent in every building Wright ever designed.

From nature and elemental geometry grew Wright's ability to abstract natural forms—reducing a flower or leaf to pure geometric shapes. This pattern could then be manipulated in various combinations into a new composition. These geometric exercises became the sources of floor plans, elevations, and decorative arts, each element generated from the same design theme. Once converted into three-dimensional forms, the elements would all work together in harmony like the natural shapes that were their source. Each building was given its own lexicon of forms, a language then used throughout the design. The art glass related to the furniture, which related to the moldings, which related to the floor plan, which related to the site plan. They became inextricably linked through geometry.

Abstracted natural motifs were used for art glass window designs in the early houses. Sometimes, a specific plant was selected, such as the tulip in the 1895 playroom of his own home in Oak Park or the sumac in the Dana-Thomas house of 1904. But in other commissions, such as the May house of 1908 in Grand Rapids, Michigan, a more generic plant form appears to be the source.

A thematic, geometric design was cast into the concrete blocks that Wright first introduced in California about 1920. In the Freeman house alone are fifty-two versions of the block design, which apparently is based on an abstraction of the site plan with a grove of eucalyptus. The variations of this basic design were repeated over and over and when massed into walls create a pattern and rhythm of their own.

In 1936 Wright designed his first Usonian house, a word he used to describe buildings uniquely suitable for life in the United States. In these houses, the abstractions are even clearer than in his early Prairie Style designs. Each home was based on a geometric grid used both in plan and in elevation. The two-by-four-foot rectangular module of the first Jacobs residence in Madison, Wisconsin, was drawn on the architectural plans as well as scored into the concrete floor. The module, or unit of design, selected for a particular building would twist and turn and be repeated over and over in the floor plan and elevations. Squares, hexagons, circles, parallelograms, and triangles also were used at different times as the basis for building designs.

Opposite: The May house windows are typical of the simply divided panels Wright used to complement natural forms outside while repeating a house's architectural forms. Wheatlike clusters rise from rectangular piers, flanked by horizontal ledge shapes. A set of Froebel blocks underneath this window shows one of Wright's formative architectural inspirations from childhood. "I sat at the little kindergarten tabletop," he later reflected, "and played...with the cube, the sphere, and the triangle. I learned to see this way and when I did, I did not care to draw casual incidentals of Nature. I wanted to design." [John Boucher, Steelcase]

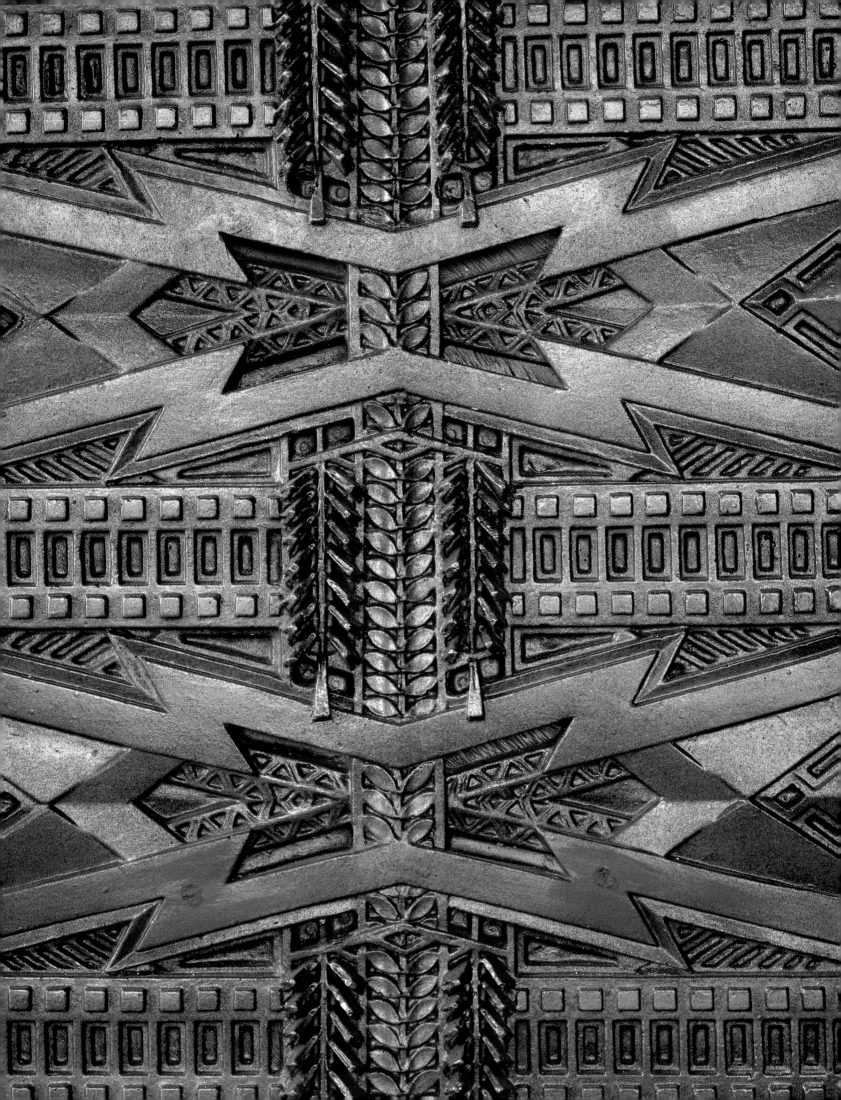

Opposite: Wright learned about integral ornament from his early employer, Louis Sullivan. Wright, however, applied a more geometrical structure to his designs such as the bronze-green, plaster frieze that surrounds the Dana-Thomas house in Springfield, Illinois. The sumac plant, used elsewhere in the house, was abstracted here to become the design's central figure.

Below: At a time when Victorian, excessively ornate houses dominated the domestic scene, Wright looked to simplicity as more meaningful and visually rewarding. He found inspiration in Japanese architecture, which may have influenced his use of sheltering, low-pitched, upturned roofs in the Dana-Thomas house. [Photographs © Judith Bromley]

LOUIS SULLIVAN

Wright moved to Chicago from his native Wisconsin in 1887, leaving the University of Wisconsin after only two semesters. He first apprenticed with Joseph Lyman Silsbee, who was actively introducing the Shingle Style to the Midwest. Within a year, Wright began his tenure at the side of Louis Sullivan, whom he would thereafter refer to as his *lieber Meister* (beloved master). Sullivan also inspired Wright to look at nature's rhythms and processes and to create architecture that related to contemporary life. Sullivan, the philosophical father of what became known as the Prairie School, provided the rhetoric that called for an American architecture that was not bound by tradition. More practically, he taught Wright about ornament. Rather than applied, he believed, it should be integral to the building itself. Wright learned from Sullivan that the elements of a building could provide all of the ornamentation that was needed. Again the refrain that governed Wright's work—simplicity, unity, nature.

JAPANESE DESIGN

Wright also was profoundly influenced by Japanese design. His first exposure was the imperial Japanese exhibit at the World's Columbian Exposition in Chicago in 1893. Known as the Ho-ho-den, its fluid spaces were covered by a broad, sheltering roof, with generous overhanging eaves. Light poured in from all sides. The walls moved, opening up spaces, releasing the box. This experience provided more data for Wright's creative mind to devour and synthesize.

The simplicity of Japanese design also revealed itself in Japanese wood-block prints, which combined his love of nature and the pureness of geometry. His fascination with them began as a young man. When he and his first wife, Catherine, visited Japan for the first time in 1905, he was able to study Japanese architecture and roam the back alleys in search of prints. At various times in his life, his impressive collection of Japanese art was sold to pay debts, and at other periods it grew to include screens, kimonos, ceramics, and textiles. But the print remained as a symbol of simplicity and elimination of all that was unnecessary. This quality provided such a pivotal impact on his design aesthetic that he published his first book, *The Japanese Print,* on the subject in 1910.

ORGANIC ARCHITECTURE

Through years of careful, intuitive observation, study, and experimentation, Wright was able to translate his unique concept of architecture into a total design ideology that he called organic architecture. He welcomed opportunities to articulate this ideology in lectures and ·publications throughout his life. Perhaps the act of organizing his thoughts and communicating them so frequently helped instill them so securely in his own behavior that the architectural consistency was sure to follow—it may have been the synthesizing process that pulled it all together. His work embodied his ideals. He truly created a new architectural language.

In 1894, at age twenty-seven, he is thought to have conceived a famous essay, "In the Cause of Architecture," that was ultimately published in *The Architectural Record* in 1908. In the essay, he set forth propositions that established an enduring grammar for his work and that of his followers. Here is a summary of this advice, which included some very specific suggestions:

☐ "Simplicity and repose are the qualities that measure the true value of any work of art." Limit the number of rooms and spaces to only what is needed. Openings should be seen as part of the structure. Eliminate unnecessary detail and ornament (for example, use a piece of wood without an extra molding, a plain wooden slat rather than a turned baluster, plain fabrics and floor coverings). Build in unsightly appliances and equipment. Use pictures only as part of an overall scheme. Build in as much furniture as possible. Consider the whole as an integral unit. Use simple unbroken wall surfaces from the water table to the roof (or the frieze below the roof).

☐ Each home should express the owners' individuality and be unique.

The Robie house of 1908 in Chicago's Hyde Park neighborhood is a masterful example of Wright's concept of organic architecture. The low hipped roof, broad overhangs, Roman brick courses, and limestone planters and copings create layers of horizontal lines that accent bold masonry masses. [Balthazar Korab]

☐ A building should appear to grow easily from its site. Design gently sloping roofs (low-pitch hipped, unbroken; low with pediments on long ridges; or a simple slab). Keep proportions low. Use suppressed heavy chimneys. Build sheltering overhangs. Include low terraces. Construct garden walls that reach out.

☐ Use natural colors. "Go to the woods and fields for color schemes." Choose warm, soft tones of earth and autumn. Do not select pessimistic blues, purples, or cool colors of the "ribbon counter."

☐ Bring out the nature of materials. Use natural wood finishes. Show the natural texture of plaster with stain applied to it. Reveal the friendly and beautiful nature of all materials.

☐ Put the machine to work to serve civilization. Maximize its usefulness (for example, use furniture with clean-cut, straight-line forms).

☐ Eliminate the boxlike compartments we live in. Open up the spaces.

☐ Group windows in a rhythmic way. Use casement windows, not double-hung, guillotine-style windows.

☐ Create floor plans in an axial and balanced order. Conceive room designs in three dimensions.

☐ Provide a place for natural foliage or flowers. Use urns, planters, garden walls.

☐ Use ornamentation that is of the building. Ornament is "constitutional" and begins with the building's conception. Create art glass windows with straight-line patterns that suit the characteristics of the glass and metal components.

☐ Determine one form for a particular building and adhere to that motif throughout the building, designing every detail of the whole.

☐ As it grows older, a house with character will grow more valuable than one that is merely in "fashion."

☐ Above all, strive for integrity.

These concepts were the fundamentals of Wright's style. Certainly, they were the marks of his Prairie Style houses, designed from the turn of the twentieth century to the mid-teens. For six decades, Wright articulated these same principles in varying ways, but

he never deviated from them. In May 1952 he defined the terms of organic architecture for *Architectural Record* once again. He reiterated his principles, but this time the specifics related more to his Usonian houses than to their Prairie Style predecessors.

Organic architecture was definitely a new sense of shelter for *humane* life. Shelter, broad and low. Roofs, either flat or pitched, hipped or gabled, but always comprehensive Shelter. Wide flat eaves were sometimes perforated to let trellised light through upon characteristic ranges of windows below. Ornament was nonexistent unless integral. Walls became screens, often glass screens, and the new open-plan spread space upon a concrete ground mat: the whole structure intimate and wide upon and of the ground itself. This ground-mat floor eventually contained the gravity-heating system (heat rises naturally as water falls) of the spaces to be lived in: forced circulation of hot water in pipes embedded in a broken stone bed beneath the floor slabs (soon misnamed "radiant heat"). Other new techniques, new forms adapted to our inevitable machine-methods appeared in these new structures. The economics of continuity and cantilevered structure were realized. Even the walls played a new role or disappeared altogether. A new sense of space in appropriate human scale pervaded not only the structure but the life itself lived in it was broadened, made more free because of sympathetic freedom of plan and structure. The interior space to be lived in became *the reality of the whole performance.* Building as a box, was gone. The integral character of the third dimension was born to architecture.

How did Wright's philosophy translate into actual buildings? What are the unique attributes that have become so identified with him? The following sections provide an overview of the elements that define his work. At the root of each was simplicity, and from simplicity came the harmony, unity, and integrity that we today identify as Wright's own style.

To break open boxlike spaces, Wright sought ways to dissolve corners. A mitered window in the Palmer garden house in Ann Arbor, Michigan, frees the interior space so that it becomes one with the outside. This Japanese-inspired teahouse actually was designed in 1964, after Wright's death, by his apprentice John Howe. Repeating Wright's module for the house itself, this intimate structure stands as a protective shelter yet welcomes the beauty of the garden—a harmonious landscape that grew from the teahouse. In their additions, both Howe and the Palmers have perpetuated Wright's principles of organic architecture. [© Judith Bromley]

Opposite: In the May house in Grand Rapids, Michigan, Wright created a perfectly unified, harmonious composition. Entering the home, one is compressed into a hallway, then released and drawn into the openness of the living area, moving freely from one space to another. [Jon Miller, © Hedrich-Blessing. Courtesy Steelcase]

Above: The 1948 Walker house on the beach at Carmel, California, reaches out like a ship's prow—at one with its site. [Balthazar Korab]

Below: To achieve a more human scale in the Martin house in Buffalo, New York, Wright used different ceiling heights and horizontal banding. [K. C. Kratt]

THE SITE

A Wright building and its site are wedded—one cannot be considered without the other. The most committed marriage of house to site is Fallingwater near Mill Run, Pennsylvania; cantilevered over a waterfall, the house is one with the rocky terrain. Similarly, the topography, the flora and fauna, and the other natural attributes of a location as well as the characteristics of the region influenced the appearance of Wright's other buildings. Houses built on the prairie, for example, reflected the whole area's horizontality, not just aspects of the specific site. In Wright's opinion, the horizontal line was the line of repose, tranquility, and domesticity. Each building, he proclaimed, should be *of* the earth, not perched *on* it.

SPACE

"The room within is the great fact about the building," wrote Wright in 1928. This space, the reason for the building itself, dictates the exterior shape. To Wright, spaces were meant to be fluid, free flowing, and informal like the American lifestyle. In Wright houses, living spaces tend to blend together. Closed rooms are limited to bathrooms and bedrooms. He beckoned Americans to break out of their boxes, reach outside—visually, through window walls, and actually, using terraces, porches, and sensitive site planning. He also used space as a technique for controlling experiences within a building. Entrances and rooms were often narrow and confining so that the space at the end would feel more expansive. Confine-and-release proved an effective exercise in contrasts, one that provokes a subliminal awe in those who experience Wright's spaces firsthand.

SCALE

The logical source of scale in his residences was, of course, the humans who inhabited them. More often than not, however, the scale he used was his own, five feet, eight inches. The structure's proposed use and building materials also contributed to the scale chosen, but once a unit of measure was determined it became the standard for the entire building and from it grew the proportions. Doorways and ceiling heights were brought down to a more human scale, creating a feeling of comfort and oneness with the architecture.

MATERIALS

Natural materials in their natural condition and place provided inspiration for Wright's buildings. To be most effective, the number of materials was limited. Once again, simplicity. One material was always primary, while others were merely supplementary. Exterior and interior materials were often the same, just as the exterior was an expression of the interior space. Wright explored the very essence and capabilities of each type of building material so it could be most expressive in his final design. The texture inherent in the dominant material provided a "feeling," an identity. The context of a building certainly played an important role in what was chosen. City and suburban dwellings were more likely to be built of even, level, brick; asymmetrical stone was more appropriate for the countryside.

☐ Stone. Of all the materials Wright used, he probably spoke about stone the most. He had great appreciation for this ancient building material and built Taliesin, his own home in Spring Green, Wisconsin, from native limestone carried from a nearby quarry and Taliesin West from the boulders found on the Arizona desert floor.

He looked to the quarry itself for guidance on how to lay up stone. "The rock ledges of a stone-quarry are a story and a longing to me. There is a suggestion in the strata and character in the formations," he wrote in 1928. A local stonemason who worked for Wright at Taliesin for fourteen years stated it in a different way: "Frank liked that stick-out stuff," he said, referring to the alternate layers of projecting stones with barely visible mortar that mimicked the quarry strata. For nearly fifty years, Wright continued to shape, mold, expand, and define Taliesin using stone. The apprentices who studied with him learned about its properties by building walls there. Local indigenous stone was specified for numerous commissions in

different areas of the country. The results were houses clearly in sympathy with their setting.

☐ Brick. Brick in a variety of colors, finishes, and dimensions was specified throughout Wright's career and was not limited to use as an exterior building material. He saw no need to hide what many regarded as too crude a material for the living room. He not only left it exposed inside but liberally used it to define the central core of his buildings. Whether he used brick of standard proportions or the flatter, Roman style, Wright often accented the horizontality of a building by requesting custom tooling and coloring of the mortar. Vertical joints were cut flush with the brick face and colored to match the brick, but horizontal joints were deeply raked to create a long shadow. A massive masonry chimney stood at the core of the majority of his residences and served as the focal point for family life as well as the design itself.

☐ Wood. Before advances in steel fabrication technology, Wright depended primarily on wood as his principal structural element. Those currently restoring his early homes are amazed at the confidence he had in the material. Its properties were certainly stretched as his bold new designs sometimes outpaced technology. But machine technologies were put to use to cut costs and enhance the qualities of wood. Using veneers helped reduce the ecological impact on forests and saved money.

For interiors, Wright favored certain woods during different periods of his career, but they were always used with great respect for their inherent beauty. He abhorred covering the intricate, luscious patterns of wood grain with paint or concealing its linear power with

Opposite: Wright combined his favorite materials at the entrance to his Oak Park studio. Common brick dominates the design but is richly accented with limestone, wood, shingles, glass, plaster ornament, and even nature's own flowers. Despite the variety of materials, simplicity prevails. [Jon Miller, © Hedrich-Blessing]

curvaceous turning or scrollwork. Stains and shellacs were sometimes used to enhance the color of the wood, and waxes and oils were preferred over varnishes. In the early years, oak, particularly quartersawn, was dominant, although he also used other woods such as birch, walnut, and maple. Later, cypress and Philippine mahogany were used extensively. A few of the early residences and numerous Usonian houses used broad boards and battens, often of cypress, as the principal building material both inside and out. The introduction of plywood offered new possibilities, because it, too, was inexpensive, durable, and flexible.

Simple bands of wood trim, sometimes called marking strips, inside and out defined surface planes and led the eye. This technique accented the horizontality and fluidity of the open spaces Wright created, which in turn helped relate a building's scale to the inhabitants.

☐ Plaster. Plaster finishes typically had a sand float and were sometimes stained or colored, rather than painted. Wright also used special painting techniques called stippling and scumbling to further enhance wall textures; these somewhat mottled finishes tended to dissolve the solidity of the wall, giving the illusion of more openness. Additionally, he cast plaster in molds with elaborate Sullivanesque patterns and integrated these panels into several of his early buildings, designs that frequently were mistaken for terra cotta. The stork panels outside his own studio in Oak Park, Illinois, and the roofline friezes on homes such as the Winslow, Dana, Heller, and Husser houses in Illinois were some of his significant decorative elements.

☐ Stucco. This durable, inexpensive building material was repeatedly used during the Prairie Style period. While it was most often seen in

Wright's designs for affordable housing such as the "Fireproof House for $5,000" of 1906 and the Richards American System Built Homes of 1916, it was employed also in numerous larger commissions, such as the William Martin and Fricke houses in Oak Park.

☐ Concrete. Once again, Wright looked at a lowly construction material, studied its properties, and made it beautiful. Lacking the inherent beauty of other materials, concrete was redeemed by its plasticity. It was poured into monolithic walls and cantilevered terraces. It was molded into tactile blocks. It was combined with steel to create a solid fabric. It was mixed with fine sand and large rocks to create natural panels. It was colored. It was poured as a floor, covering radiant heating systems. It was used as a roof. Wright shaped it and stretched it in countless ways in his buildings for more than fifty years.

☐ Copper. The decorative potential of copper, previously viewed primarily as a durable sheet metal, included color (from blue-green to bronze) and an inherent plasticity. Beginning with the horizontal stretch of the eaves, Wright wrapped this ancient material around other features, particularly near window expanses. Its liberal use in the Coonley house in Riverside, Illinois, and May house in Grand Rapids, Michigan, emphasized certain motifs and added richness to the overall designs. Pleated copper roofs were specified on several commissions, but they were not always built because of the cost and availability.

☐ Glass. Advances in glass technology, more than any other innovation, permitted Wright to break open the box. A foil for the texture and weight of other building materials, glass served to lighten Wright's designs. It enabled him to balance solid screens with light screens so that the building would no longer have to be confining. In the Prairie Style years, his intricate, geometric art glass designs repeated building colors and patterns and provided a privacy screen for the family within. The different facets of the glass reflected light in such a way that window coverings were unnecessary in the daytime. He discovered that when mitered at a corner, glass actually dissolved the intersection. When butted into a stone wall, glass served as protection from the weather while accenting the strength and texture of the stone. Used generously, glass allowed Wright to integrate inside and outside spaces, blurring the distinction between them.

Opposite, from left to right: Some of the key materials found in Wright's buildings: a limestone wall at Taliesin [Tony Puttnam, Frank Lloyd Wright Foundation]; tulip art glass at his Oak Park home [Gordon Beall]; a concrete textile block at the Ennis house [Balthazar Korab]; stucco on the Henderson house [© Judith Bromley]; brick at the Bogk house [Eric Oxendorf]; board-and-batten siding on the Davenport house [Chester Brummel]; limestone trim and common brick at Wright's home and studio [Ann Abernathy]; decorative copper gutters on the Dana-Thomas house [© Judith Bromley]; a rubble wall at Taliesin West [Richard Maack, Adstock].

COLOR

Wright selectively drew his color schemes from nature, leaning more towards the colors of autumn in the Midwest. The inherent colors of the building materials certainly dominated and set the tone for all of his decorative schemes. The warm tans and browns of the brick, stone, and wood usually were combined with varying shades of their component hues, from red to yellow-green, producing an analogous color scheme. Most often they ranged from a warm reddish gold to a muted yellow-green. Creams, beiges, warm grays, and browns were suitable additions. The colors were relatively intense but toned down enough not to be harsh. The appearance of an organic home was harmonious and restful, a unity of form and color. The palette might include several shades of the same basic colors that were varied throughout the house. There is a noticeable absence in Wright's repertoire of pure black and white; they seem to be in bold violation of his thesis of harmony and unity. Characteristic colors remained warm and autumnal for decades. Only in his later years, when others became more involved in the interiors, did occasional clear blues and chartreuse begin to appear in his homes.

Wright's use of red became his signature. In fact, red was the color of the square signature tile that he began to place on his houses in the 1930s. His long-time associate John Howe remembers that a client, one of the Pauson sisters, was a potter and suggested creating such a tile. Wright was delighted with the idea. While many reds were used in his schemes, he preferred a warm, brownish red that he called Cherokee red. Some say the color came from a favorite native American pot, but it could just as well have been inspired by the warm red barns that dotted his rural Wisconsin homeland. That red, actually an iron oxide mixture, was used to help preserve the wood in the barn. It was a familiar and natural companion to the colors of the foliage. Wright colored his own Midway farm buildings at Taliesin Cherokee red, as well as his fleet of cars, his roofs, his gates, and his signs. It was specified as the accent color in many of his buildings and continues to be generously used by his followers. Even concrete floors were integrally colored and waxed with a warm red.

The particular shade and intensity of red vary from site to site and use to use depending on the light, the building materials, and the setting. In practice, Cherokee red is not just one color but has become a range of hues. For instance, Taliesin West, Wright's home in Scottsdale, Arizona, uses a lighter value than Taliesin in Wisconsin. Paint pigmentation and composition have changed so dramatically since Wright first began his practice that now there is a hundred times more variety than before. For environmental and stability reasons, many of the natural pigments have been replaced with synthetics. But the ability to create a rich, brownish red is still a challenge.

Wright also experimented with metallic paints and gold leaf. Walls in his own Oak Park studio entrance were painted with a bronze paint; he even proposed gold leaf for the exterior of his masterpiece, Fallingwater. He was particularly fond of gold during his Imperial Hotel era in the late teens and 1920s, no doubt borrowing it from the Japanese screens he loved. Using different methods, he laid gold in the mortar joints of the brick fireplaces of the Martin house in Buffalo, May house in Grand Rapids, and Allen house in Wichita. Certainly a product of the earth, it added a richness, an elegance, that other materials could not.

Photographs, page 40, from left to right: Wright drew his colors from nature: a California sunrise [Don Giannatti, Adstock]; limestone outcroppings near Taliesin [Tony Puttnam, Frank Lloyd Wright Foundation]; sumac leaves in the fall [Balthazar Korab]; spring prairie grasses [Balthazar Korab].

Photographs, page 41, from left to right: Wrightian red showed itself in many hues: the trim of the bell at Taliesin West [Richard Bowditch]; Wright's 1940 Lincoln [Domino's Center for Architecture and Design]; the spiral Taliesin West logo [Richard Bowditch]; Wright's red signature tile at Taliesin [Richard Bowditch].

Opposite: Wrapping around a pier between the May house hall and dining room, a shimmering hollyhock mural draws on the golds and greens of the house's color palette. It was painted by George Niedecken, who coordinated the interiors, and was recently recovered from under six layers of paint. [John Boucher, Steelcase]

LIGHT

Both natural and artificial light were partners in Wright's harmonious whole. Houses were sited to make the most of the sun's powers. Window walls were most likely on the south elevation allowing the sun to flood the rooms with light and warmth. Skylights and clerestory windows brought natural light into rooms away from open window walls. The changing quality of light in different seasons and different times of day, controlled by the shape and location of his light screens, affected life in the home.

Electricity, introduced to the Chicago area at about the time Wright was building his first home in Oak Park, offered new opportunities for integrating lighting. It was now safe to conceal light behind grillework and art glass, reflect it off ceilings, and hang it over furniture. It could augment the sun's ability to create shadows and texture. For most of his career, Wright was fond of using decks—long, deep shelves that seemed to float below the ceiling—to hide indirect light fixtures, create spatial variety, and reduce the perceived height in a room to human scale. These decks, constructed of the same material as the ceiling, usually are on the perimeter of a space, but sometimes they span openings from one room to another.

Opposite: Wright carefully used natural light. He opened the southern facade of the May house to the sun, using art glass windows that wrap around the corner and rise to skylights overhead. They dissolve the wall and obliterate the corner. In the day a warm glow fills the room. [Jon Miller, © Hedrich-Blessing. Courtesy Steelcase]

Above: At dusk on a winter day, the skylight is illuminated and the wall and table lamps in the May house are turned on—creating a different, more dramatic, glow. The art glass uses square and abstract leaf motifs found throughout the house. [Balthazar Korab]

DECORATIVE ARTS

The majority of the decorative elements in a Wright environment are designed to be part of the unified whole. Wright liked to integrate all of the arts. Furniture, light fixtures, carpets, fireplace andirons, sometimes linens and china often were augmented by sculpture, decorative grilles, screens, and murals designed for that particular site. George Niedecken, who coordinated many of Wright's interiors during the heyday of the Prairie Style years, began working with Wright as a muralist. His paintings of plants and flowers were used on the upper walls of several major commissions including the Dana, Coonley, and May residences. Marion Mahony, the only woman designer in the Oak Park studio, also was responsible for many of the early decorative art designs. Later, Gene Masselink provided masterful geometric murals that became focal points of Wright interiors. Japanese screens were sometimes recommended to clients and would be attached to or built into a wall. Perforated wood panels or concrete blocks in abstracted nature patterns were used as screens for natural and artificial light. Two outstanding examples of ceiling grilles are in Wright's Oak Park home, one in the playroom and the other in the dining room (page 17). Nearly every Usonian house had its own geometric, perforated grille pattern that created shadows in the appropriate motif throughout the home.

Right: The art glass skylight in Wright's Oak Park studio is one of his most complex designs. He used such panels in ceilings and windows as decorative elements, as a means of diffusing light, and as a visual picture frame. Their varied facets reflect light during the day so that windows can be uncovered yet private. [Chester Brummel]

Opposite, left to right: A montage of decorative arts from Wright's creative treasury: scumbling, a multiple-step painting technique, Dana-Thomas house [© Judith Bromley]; brick fireplace with golden glass in the mortar joints, May house [John Boucher, Steelcase]; textured upholstery fabric, Zimmerman house [Michael Komanecky]; lighted textile block, Freeman house [John Marshall]; bronze sconce, May house [John Boucher, Steelcase]; Sullivanesque master bedroom stencil detail, Wright's Oak Park home [Chester Brummel]; geometric carpet design, May house [John Boucher, Steelcase]; dining room chair, Wright's Oak Park home [© Judith Bromley]; plywood Usonian furniture detail, Zimmerman house [Michael Komanecky].

 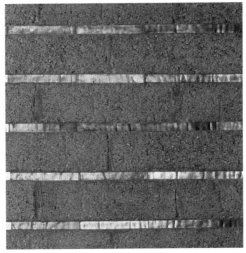 

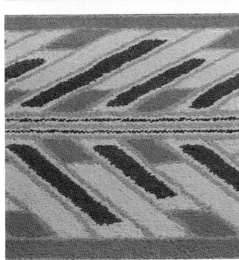  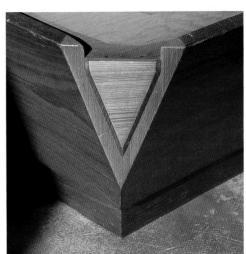

FURNITURE

Wright began to design furniture for his buildings as he was formulating his concepts of organic architecture. First, in the 1880s and 1890s, he adopted the conventional mode by building in some cabinets and shelving. Soon he added seating units around fireplaces and in hallways. Then in 1895 he designed his own dining room table and chairs, possibly his first free-standing furniture. His concept of a totally integrated, harmonious interior required that he design more and more furniture for his buildings, because there was little on the market that had the rectilinear simplicity required to fulfill his vision. But the extent to which Wright actually designed pieces for the early houses varied, probably based on the willingness of clients to either spend the money or submit to his ideas.

In some of the Prairie houses, he designed built-in cabinets and possibly a bench, a large dining or library table, and maybe some chairs. These would be mixed with more ornate pieces owned by the client. As his concepts and his ability to persuade clients matured, he was able to design more and more elements so that the furniture was barely distinguishable from the building itself, as can be seen in the later Prairie and Usonian houses; the furniture was made of the same materials, same finishes, same details and proportions. The clients who moved into his houses often were forced to leave their old furniture behind. They neither needed it nor wanted it to interfere with the unity of their new homes.

His furniture styles thus evolved, just as his architectural vocabulary changed. The solid rectilinear oak pieces of the Prairie era became lighter and then more Oriental in feeling as his architectural interests shifted. The economical simplicity of the Usonian houses called for basic furniture, built of plywood, presumably constructed on site by the carpenters but usually by local cabinetmakers. The versatility of the pieces, in addition to their inherent suitablity to the spaces, makes it hard to imagine one without the other.

In 1955 Wright created a line of furniture for the Heritage-Henredon Furniture Company, thus opening his creativity to those who did not own a Wright-designed home. While this may seem to be a compromise in his ideals, the line was based on the same principles as his house-specific furniture. Using basic circular, rectilinear, and triangular shapes, most of the seventy-five mahogany pieces were modular, so that they could adapt to different settings. They were simple and functional, with the ornament integral—not applied to it.

TEXTILES

Textiles that Wright selected were simple and natural—no heavy brocades or elaborate floral prints. Instead, he preferred simple linens, cottons, and wools in flat weaves or fine, short-napped velvets. He was known to assist in the actual design of a particular weave of upholstery or drapery fabric. Textiles were used to complement or accentuate the surrounding texture of a room. In the first few decades, satin-weave wools, velvets, and tightly woven linens seemed to be the dominant choices. Eventually, more handwoven and nubbier textures provided contrast for the smoother Usonian houses. When a pattern was used, it was geometric and related to the overall motif of the building. Leather was a popular chair covering, and an occasional animal skin was added to provide variety in textures. Each textile became one more unit that contributed to the integrity of the whole.

Influenced by the Arts and Crafts movement near the turn of the century, and encouraged by the needlework ability of the wife of one of his designers, George Niedecken, Wright included custom-designed linens in several of his Prairie Style houses. Patterns used in the table and bed scarves again were drawn from the house's dominating geometric motif.

Carpets and floor coverings also were simple and made of natural fibers. Wright or one of his associates, such as George Niedecken or Marion Mahony, custom designed woven carpets for some of the Prairie houses. As part of the unified whole, they served to pull together the geometric motifs and colors that were used elsewhere in the home. Current reproductions are often tufted but, if properly done, can provide the same appearance as the historic weaves. In some of the later homes, woven linen, jute, and wool mats were chosen, providing a textured foil for the smooth concrete floors. Geometric Oriental, native American, and Scandinavian rugs and weavings also were widely used, allowing owners to personalize their homes with their textile collections.

The 1908 Robie house commission gave Wright the opportunity to design many decorative arts, including numerous pieces of oak furniture and carpeting. The shape of the sofa, with its unique table arms, echoes the ceiling above it. The trim on the furniture matches the moldings on the walls, creating free-standing architectural elements in a totally unified space. [Jon Miller, © Hedrich-Blessing]

ACCEΣΣORIEΣ

Free-standing accessories most compatible with Wright interiors tend to be somewhat geometric and nature oriented. Tree branches and boughs, usually evergreens, are brought inside and spread overhead across light decks, on shelves, and on tabletops in both of Wright's Taliesins. Simple, natural bouquets of seasonal flowers or dried weeds fill geometric vases. Arts and Crafts, native American, pre-Columbian, and contemporary pottery fit easily into his geometric schemes. Certain Arts and Crafts ceramics and metalware also work comfortably in a Wright interior. Items with solid matte finishes and geometric shapes are most compatible. The blue-green color of Teco pottery is a nice complement to the warm tones preferred by the architect.

Wright-designed spaces can accommodate sculptures more readily than paintings because of the limited amount of open wall space. This deliberate rejection of most two-dimensional art excluded his beloved Japanese prints, which he stored and exhibited on specially designed print tables or easels.

Wright's care in selecting accessories was the culmination of the attention he gave to every aspect of his houses, from fitting the form to the site, selecting the materials, and using natural inspirations wherever he found them. His organic architecture speaks to the values of today's society even more accurately than it did at the turn of the century. In a hectic, complex, impersonal world that is being forced to look at the lessons of nature to save the planet, there is great relevance in Wright's teachings. His designs were based on simplicity, the dignity of the individual, and, above all, an abiding respect for nature.

At the Dana house, Wright called on Richard Bock to provide sculptures to suit the grand spaces. Bock's *The Flower in the Crannied Wall* stands at the entry, greeting guests. Wright worked closely with Bock, Alfonso Iannelli, and George Niedecken in his early years to integrate works of art into his houses. [© Judith Bromley]

Opposite: At the Hollyhock house, the Los Angeles residence Wright designed for arts patron Aline Barnsdall, he created decorative wooden torchieres as part of the sofa. Behind the high-back chair is a Japanese screen, one of his favorite accessories; its metallic gold background is repeated in the wall finish. [© Alexander Vertikoff]

WRIGHT'S OWN HOMES

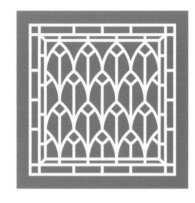

THERE IS NO BETTER WAY TO EXPERIENCE THE GENIUS OF WRIGHT'S DESIGN ABILITY THAN TO EXPLORE THE PLACES IN WHICH HE LIVED. HIS THREE HOMES STAND AS COMPLETE EXPRESSIONS OF ORGANIC ARCHITECTURE — FROM THREE PERSPECTIVES OF THE MASTER HIMSELF.

Previous pages: A blazing fire in one of many fireplaces at Taliesin, Wright's Wisconsin home, conveys the power of the hearth—the center of Wright houses. Here, tea is prepared for guests on a cool afternoon. The gnarled driftwood and wrought-iron fixtures, so carefully placed, complete the cavelike setting. [Richard Bowditch]

Opposite: Client presentations were made in the octagonal library in Wright's Oak Park studio. Here, protected from distraction, in a deliberately controlled space, he held clients in rapt attention. The unity of the space, with its oak furniture and selected artifacts, was an advertisement for his creativity. [Jon Miller, © Hedrich-Blessing]

HOME AND STUDIO

In 1889 twenty-one-year-old Frank Lloyd Wright borrowed $5,000 from his employer, Louis Sullivan, to build a six-room bungalow for himself and his new eighteen-year-old bride, Catherine Tobin. For the next twenty years, he shaped this building in Oak Park, Illinois, in response to the changing needs of his family and his emerging design philosophy. Like his future homes, Taliesin and Taliesin West, it became his laboratory. Here he could safely experiment with new concepts that he further developed in his commissions.

While compact, the house already discloses Wright's desire to break out of traditional boxlike rooms. Doorways were widened or eliminated so space could flow freely, allowing the rooms to seem larger and less confining. Simple oak bands wrap around the walls, leading the eye from room to room and providing a human scale.

The walls of the house conveyed the feeling of movable screens rather than solid walls, even before the Japanese pavilion at the Columbian Exposition in 1893 could have affected his attitude toward space. These solid screens, contrasted with window group-ings that serve as light screens, make the living spaces feel flexible and open, suitable for a growing family's needs. Wright had not begun to design his own art glass windows when the house was built. Thus, he selected a simple geometric diamond pattern that created only a minor transitional barrier between the inside and the outside. The walls were starting to dissolve.

Frank and Catherine furnished their home with antiques bought at auctions in the area until Wright began to design his own furniture. A mixture of exotic wood tables and cabinets, an upright piano, palms, and a patchwork of Oriental rugs fill the rooms. Velvet upholstered built-in seating areas are beneath the windows. The family's exuberance was apparent in their unconventional home.

By 1895 the Wrights had four active children who needed more space. A large addition was built adjoining the east side of the house. It includes two brilliantly articulated and integrated spaces: the barrel-vaulted playroom (pages 6–7) and a new dining room (page 17) where the former kitchen had been. These new rooms demon-strated how far Wright had come artistically in just six years. His principles of organic architecture, written the year before, were firmly in place. The rooms were functionally responsive, geometri-cally pure, and partners with nature. Both have wooden fretwork panels in the ceiling in abstracted nature patterns. The playroom

screen has a skylight, and the dining room has a recessed electric light, a first. Like branches overhead, they shelter but open the spaces above. The light fixtures and furniture were built as components of the architecture. It is a totally unified environment. Other spaces on both floors shifted their uses slightly now that the family could stretch out a bit. The old dining room became the study. Wright's studio became the bedroom for all of the children.

Within three years Wright decided to integrate his work and home life. The studio addition was constructed, advertising his revolutionary ideas to all. To the triangular-shaped home he added a complex, geometric composition of rectangles, octagons, and squares. It includes a drafting room with a balcony, his office, a library, and an impressive reception hall. Long, low brick walls stretch across the entire facade, unifying all of the elements. Two sculptures of bent human figures, columns with integrated molded plaster panels, and huge planted urns designate the mazelike entrance (page 35).

The richness continues inside the studio. The low ceiling of the metallic bronze-colored reception hall includes three long, intricate art glass panels (page 44). Light filters through their gold and green geometric designs, abstractions from nature. To the left is the octagonal drafting room, and to the right is the octagonal library. Straight ahead is Wright's office, where art glass panels filter natural light from overhead and frame a garden view. Everywhere one looks are stimulating new architectural ideas and lush decorative arts.

Today, the restored spaces appear just as they were when Wright lived and worked there. The building now is owned by the National Trust for Historic Preservation and operated by the Frank Lloyd Wright Home and Studio Foundation.

Above: Seen here from the study, the living room is light-filled from expanses of simple diamond-paned windows or "light screens." Wright streamlined the furnishings with built-in seats. The colors—like the earth itself—are darker at the base and lighten as the eye moves upward, from oak to cream. [Jon Miller, © Hedrich-Blessing]

Opposite below: The original six-room, Shingle Style bungalow, with its sheltering roof and extended garden wall, was later joined by the studio at left. [Donald G. Kalec]

Left: The inglenook presides over an intimate alcove, a contrast to the overall feeling of spaciousness. A polygonal cabinet echoes nearby bay windows. [Chester Brummel]

Studio activity centered on the two-story drafting room. An octagon on a cube, with a balcony suspended by chains above the work area, it was revolutionary in its space and materials. Here Wright and his eager apprentices poured out 162 building designs over thirteen whirlwind years. [Jon Miller, © Hedrich-Blessing]

Earth tones in Wright's studio office created a muted yet welcoming retreat. Natural light, diffused through colored panels, came in from a skylight overhead and art glass windows to the side. The straight lines of the modern chair contrast nicely with Japanese prints, textiles, and dried weeds in pottery vases. [Chester Brummel]

TALIESIN

Wright left the Oak Park home in 1909, first traveling to Europe to assist with the publication of his work by German publisher Ernst Wasmuth. A former client, Mamah Borthwick Cheney, accompanied him. Both had decided to leave their spouses and begin a new chapter in their lives. On his return to the United States two years later, Anna Lloyd Wright convinced her son that he should take over her property near the family enclave in Spring Green, Wisconsin.

In 1911 he began plans for a home there that would be "of the hill, not on the hill," one that overlooked the Wisconsin River and the land of his Welsh forebears. He named it Taliesin, which means "shining brow" in Welsh and was also the name of a famous Welsh poet. Taliesin was designed to be a self-sufficient farm, not just a home. The limestone and sand-colored stucco walls stretched across the hill, enclosing farm buildings, studio space, and courtyards as well as living space. This was the beginning of a remarkable complex that suffered several major fires and was rebuilt and remodeled continuously as Wright perfected his own environment over the next forty-eight years.

Today, Taliesin is a beautifully created community of organic buildings. The original home and studio of approximately 7,000 square feet have grown to some 37,000 square feet, plus three-quarters as much in gardens, courts, and terraces. Nestled neatly, under broad sheltering roofs, on other parts of the 600 rolling acres are the Hillside Home School buildings, Tan-y-deri (his sister's house), several other smaller residences, the Midway farm buildings, and the Romeo and Juliet windmill (a Wright design from 1896). A dammed-up stream on the valley floor creates a waterfall and pond 100 feet below the home. Surrounding vegetable gardens provide food for the Taliesin Fellowship, an apprenticeship-based architecture school that still resides at Taliesin, particularly during the warm months.

The house is really a series of connected buildings joined by roofed passageways and courtyards. The transition from outside to inside is smooth and deliberate. The covered courtyard at the entrance gradually becomes the foyer within the home, the limestone floor continuing. Once inside, the compressed foyer space is released into the great expanse of the living room to the left. The ceiling follows the roofline two stories up, but the room is decidedly horizontal and tranquil in feeling. The interplay of spaces, textures, light, and color draws one into the room. New discoveries are around

each corner: a massive fireplace, a tiny alcove, a place to sit and reflect, a place to listen to music, a place to visit with friends.

A narrow, forty-foot balcony is cantilevered into the treetops for better viewing of the natural life below. The limestone walls, where exposed, are laid with alternating rows of projecting stones, like the quarries from which they came. The sand and golden plaster walls are divided by cypress bands into horizontal panels that serve as backdrops for a panoply of decorative arts. The geometry of the custom-designed furniture, art glass, and carpets complements the natural vistas framed by the windows (pages 4–5). Selected pieces of Oriental art are scattered throughout Taliesin, some actually cemented into place as permanent, integral parts of the building.

To the right of the foyer flow a guest room, a loggia, a garden room, and private bedrooms of the Wrights. Above and below are more guest quarters. Each room has a thoughtfully crafted fireplace on a principal wall. These are the only heat sources for most of the building but serve to radiate the essential beauty of the stone as much as the heat. Most of the openings are vertical or oversized. In some the top stone is laid on its side; others are open from two sides. Ceiling heights change from room to room, redefining the spaces for their particular use. Doors and windows frequently open onto balconies, cantilevered observation decks, or terraces, continuing the flow of space. Most of the rooms are oriented to the east, bringing the morning light into the composition. The harmony within each room and among rooms leaves a feeling of inner tranquility.

Wright's studio adjoins the home through a covered walkway. It was his private atelier, where he welcomed clients and discussed his visions that would change their lives. A decorative panel from Sullivan's Auditorium Building hangs on the limestone wall, and a Buddha looks on from above. Natural grasses brought in from the surrounding field fill earthen pots. [Richard Bowditch]

Following pages: The living room is one of the most memorable spaces in America. The drama of its soaring multilevel spaces; the tactile variety of the stone, plaster, and wood surfaces; the artistry in the furniture; the golden tones; the genius of the composition are all intrinsically Wrightian. Barrel chairs repeat circular shapes in the carpet beneath them. [© Yukio Futagawa]

Above: Until 1998 the tea circle in the garden court was sheltered by an ancient oak tree, which fell in a summer storm. In this outdoor room the Wrights gathered with their apprentices and guests for afternoon tea. It was a restful space that conveyed his most elemental beliefs in the power of simplicity, geometry, and nature. [Pedro E. Guerrero]

Left: The garden gate, made of iron pipe painted Cherokee red, is a linear composition that serves as a counterpoint to vines and flowers. [Richard Bowditch]

Opposite: From across a pond, the earth-colored Taliesin appears out of the greenery like a treehouse. Designed to be *of* the hill, not *on* it, the long, low building stretches across the brow of the hill. From its rooms, Wright could view the rolling river valley farms that were settled by his forebears. Reflected in the water, Taliesin seems at one with nature. Apprentices of the Taliesin Fellowship, founded here in 1932, work down the hill in the large drafting room that once was the Hillside Home School, which Wright's aunts had operated. [Richard Bowditch]

TALIESIN WEST

By 1932 Wright had founded the Taliesin Fellowship, whose apprentices shared all aspects of life at Taliesin. Cooking, gardening, scrubbing, partying, playing music, and entertaining were all as much a part of the communal life as the architectural tasks. Like Wright's spaces, his unified lifestyle did not compartmentalize daily life. Wright and his third wife, Olgivanna, decided in 1937 that the Wisconsin winters were too unbearable for year-round occupancy. Taliesin was not centrally heated and thus was insufferable in the subzero cold.

In 1928 Wright and some apprentices built near Phoenix, Arizona, a canvas-covered camp, Ocatillo, that in some ways became the prototype for Taliesin West. They later found a beautiful mesa just below McDowell Peak near Scottsdale that was perfect for their permanent architectural camp. Construction of the winter home for the fellowship, which then numbered about thirty people, began in 1937.

Wright described Taliesin West in his 1943 autobiography.

Plans were inspired by the character and beauty of that wonderful site. . . . Just imagine what it would be like on top of the world looking over the Universe at sunrise or at sunset with clear sky in between. Light and air bathing all the worlds of creation in all the color that ever was— all the shapes and outlines ever devised . . . all beyond the reach of the human mind. . . . For the designing of our buildings, certain forms already abounded. There were simple characteristic silhouettes to go by, tremendous drifts and heaps of sunburned desert rocks were nearby to be used. . . . From first to last, thousands of cords of stone, carloads of cement, carloads of redwood, acres of stout white canvas doubled over wood frames four feet by eight feet. . . . We devised a light canvas covered redwood framework resting upon this massive stone masonry that belonged to the mountain slopes all around. On a fair day, when these white tops and side flaps were flung open, the desert air and the birds flew clear through.

Opposite: Wright's western retreat drew its triangular motif from the surrounding mountain profiles, a unity of building and site. The solidity of the masonry base contrasts with the airiness of the top. Appearing both anchored and adrift, the good ship Taliesin West projects confidence and adventure. Ancient boulders with native American petroglyphs were relocated to prominent places. [Richard Maack, Adstock]

Left: The patterns of the angular redwood forms are most apparent in the drafting room, now covered with plastic. [Balthazar Korab]

Following pages: The garden room was used by the family, for fellowship gatherings, for a constant stream of guests, and for frequent musical concerts. The "butterfly" chairs, like folded origami, repeat the triangular theme of the room. [© Yukio Futagawa]

Like Taliesin, Taliesin West was ever-evolving and changed as the needs of the fellowship changed. The canvas roofs were rearranged, rebuilt, and eventually replaced with various synthetic materials that were more durable but permitted the same translucent light. Glass, not allowed in the early plans, was added in greater and greater quantities beginning in 1945. Spaces were added and made more permanent. Three rooms—Wright's private office, the drafting room, and the garden room—were the original canvas-covered spaces. They joined a dining room, a kitchen, Wright's private quarters to the east, and an apprentices court to the north.

Also like Taliesin, Taliesin West is actually many separate buildings linked together by partially covered walkways, courtyards, and terraces, all surrounded by native vegetation. Moving through the complex, one is guided, but not controlled. Even the steps are gentle, broad, and shallow, more horizontal than vertical. Shadows link the architectural elements and furniture, repeating the angular, rhythmic lines of the mountains behind. The trellised pergola along the drafting room leaves a pattern on the ground below. The natural colors, from mauve to an orange-red, are accentuated by the blooming vegetation. This does not appear to be a barren desert but a lush one, rich with natural wonders, enhanced by skillful management of its resources.

Everywhere, breathtaking vistas and fascinating close-up views are framed. The rugged textures and open informal spaces seem both primitive, like the original camp, and yet sophisticated. The contrasts abound: the simplicity and the grandeur; the smooth and the rough; the light and the heavy; the narrow and the expansive; the regular and the irregular, the natural and the built; cool blue with warm pinks. Each element was made greater by the other.

Above: Water—splashing, cooling, reflecting—became an integral design element here, a dramatic and soothing contrast to the desert dryness. The triangular pool repeats the complex's main theme. This 1937 view shows the camplike winter headquarters soon after it was built. [Hedrich-Blessing, Chicago Historical Society]

Opposite and right: The unusual, battered rubble walls, inside and out, were created because all of the large desert stones seemed to have one flat side. Rather than cut them to shape, Wright—always experimenting—decided to use their flat, colorful side out, sideways, in a bed of formed concrete. [Ezra Stoller, © Esto]

CLASSIC WRIGHT HOUSES

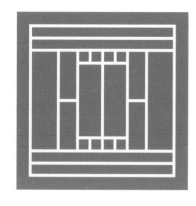

WHETHER DESIGNED TO ALIGN WITH THE PRAIRIE, PROJECT OVER A WATERFALL, RECALL ANCIENT MAYANS, OR PROVIDE AN ECONOMICAL HOME PERFECT FOR AMERICAN LIVING — THESE CLASSIC HOUSES CONVEY THE ESSENCE OF THE ENVIRONMENTS WRIGHT CREATED.

Opposite: Wright gave Susan Lawrence Dana an extraordinary dining room and gallery in which to entertain governors, politicians, and other notable guests. The dramatic barrel-vaulted ceiling in the Springfield, Illinois, house repeats the grand arch over the main entry. A stylized mural of sumac and other foliage, painted by George Niedecken, surrounds the upper walls of the dining room, furthering the feeling of being in a forest glen—with lights as fanciful as butterflies. Sometimes as many as forty chairs were grouped around the dining table, alternating high and low versions and creating a mini-room within the larger room. Here as elsewhere in the house, special benches invited one to sit in more intimate areas. Print tables allowed close study of art in the gallery. Music was always a lively ingredient of Dana's dinners, parties, and charitable events. When the house was commissioned in 1902, it was the largest residence Wright had ever undertaken. [© Judith Bromley]

PRAIRIE STYLE

Wright's early experiments with historic styles and his life experiences coalesced into a grammar of forms that became known as the Prairie School of architecture—not an education center but a school of thought. The Prairie Style was an attempt by Wright and a group of other young Chicago architects to create an architecture that suited the American lifestyle and landscape. Louis Sullivan contributed much of the initial philosophical enthusiasm, but Wright was the most famous Prairie School practitioner.

Some say that the style was definitively launched by the publication of Wright's design for "A Home in a Prairie Town" in the *Ladies' Home Journal* in February 1901. This strongly horizontal plan for a house with a low sheltering roof, bands of art glass windows, stucco walls with wood banding, and outreaching garden walls had many of the features that characterized this version of Wright's organic architecture. In one of his first commissions after this plan was published, the house for Susan Lawrence Dana, Wright brought to bear most of the devices he ultimately used to express organic architecture. For the next ten years he refined, refitted, and reinterpreted this memorable style in scores of residences. After that, it no longer dominated his architectural designs, but the grammar was not lost. Even Lucille and Isadore Zimmerman's house of 1950 exhibits many Prairie Style elements.

Over time most of the following Prairie Style houses, designed in Wright's early years, have maintained, or retained through authentic restorations, their purity and unity.

The May house in Grand Rapids, Michigan, one of Wright's mature Prairie designs, incorporates all of the components of the style. The architecture expresses the open, enchanting spaces within the home. The low-pitched roof, broad overhanging eaves, and linear masonry walls anchor the building to its site. But Wright proceeded to engage the land even more by recessing the home eighteen inches below grade and further shortening the perceived building height with a knee-high hedge on the earthen berms. Garden walls, planters, terraces, and balconies stretch the interior spaces beyond their walls. Bold geometric details around the windows is reminiscent of Mayan forms. Squares within squares are wrapped in bronze-toned copper. [Jon Miller, © Hedrich-Blessing. Courtesy Steelcase]

DANA-THOMAS HOUSE

Susan Lawrence Dana, a wealthy heiress and recent widow, commissioned Wright to create an extravagant place for living and entertaining in Springfield, Illinois. The resulting thirty-five-room mansion, completed in 1904, was an imaginative and complex symphony of color and form.

Strong geometric shapes introduced outside (pages 26–27) are a preview of the varied spaces on the interior. And varied they are: ceiling levels that change dramatically within rooms, compressing then releasing; balconies to look up at and down from; hidden alcoves and nooks to be discovered; stages for musicians; a bowling alley and a billiard room. Imagination and adventure are everywhere. Generous wood bands wrap up, down, and around the walls and sometimes span spaces as light decks to further define and unite the areas. Every space, every surface, every view is carefully composed to be a unified part of the luscious whole.

Inside is a magical kingdom. Intricate art glass sparkles all around, creating subtle screens. The complex interplay of thousands of facets of glass produces a reflected light that makes the house appear jewel-like. Autumnal colors used in the glass were applied also to the textured plaster walls with a multiple-step process called scumbling, which left the walls mottled like dappled sunlight, intensifying the glow of the spaces (page 9). Tawny golds, olive greens, and burnished oranges are paired with an unusually reddish stain on the wood. It is polychromatic yet retains a unified tonal quality like a forest on a sunny fall day. In the absence of natural vegetation on the site, Wright chose to be particularly effusive with his ornament.

Dana left her home in 1928, and it remained empty until purchased by the Thomas Publishing Company in 1944. Now owned by the state of Illinois, it has been meticulously brought back to life.

The solid, rectilinear furniture echoes the scale and proportions of the rooms. Oak tables and seating pieces are trimmed and finished in the same manner as the wood moldings on the walls and ceilings. Nearly a hundred furniture pieces were designed, along with carpets, sculptures (page 49), and murals. [© Judith Bromley]

Following pages: The principal windows in the house are a geometric interpretation of sumac, whose angular shapes became the unifying theme for all of the art glass designs. The generous budget permitted four hundred fifty custom-designed art glass panels and two hundred light fixtures. [© Yukio Futagawa]

MARTIN HOUSE

Between 1902 and 1904, Wright managed to break away from Sullivanesque ornamentation and simplify his designs even more. The Darwin D. Martin residence in Buffalo, New York, while a more elaborate commission than the Dana house, was less lavishly ornamented. This entire complex for the president of the Larkin Company included a house for his sister and brother-in-law, as well as the Martins' home, garage, and conservatory. Introduced to Wright by his brother, William Martin, an Oak Park client, Darwin Martin became one of Wright's greatest patrons. Over the years, the Martin brothers were responsible for nine major commissions. Darwin Martin also responded to Wright's periodic financial troubles with some desperately needed cash at crucial times.

The Martin house spaces are purely rectilinear, based on a strict, rectangular unit of design. Every element of the composition—windows, walls, furniture, floor plan, piers, moldings—repeats the same proportions, creating an internal, harmonious rhythm. Here Wright truly broke out of the box. Only the lower half of the exterior window walls outlines the building's shape. The low-pitch, hipped roofs float above, with only a shadow leading to the set-back

windows beneath them. Strong vertical brick piers on the facade support the broad stretches of roof, freeing the walls from any structural responsibility. Standing like sentinels, they point to the dominant horizontality of the design.

Inside, more Roman brick piers support light decks that stretch from room to room, passing and intersecting the complex pattern of finely detailed wood moldings (page 33). The gold-filled, deeply raked mortar joints of the brickwork reflect light, floating the courses of brick one above the other. All first-floor living spaces open generously into each other, offering long views from one to another. Through exquisite geometric windows, natural life in the garden, oversized planters, and the conservatory could be viewed—some nearby, some at a distance.

Wright produced dozens of custom furnishing designs for the Martins, including light fixtures, rugs, and even a grand piano. Most of the sturdy oak pieces repeated the dominant rectangular theme, but the circle became an important counterpoint. While loyal to his rectangular module, Wright had an uncanny sense about the need for variety and contrast to provide relief.

The Martins shared Wright's love of nature. He gave them a conservatory and pergola, both now lost, and niches for greenery such as this typically Wrightian urn with flowers. Many art glass patterns once graced windows, doors, and skylights, only some of which remain today. The State University of New York at Buffalo has owned the house for twenty-five years and is pursuing a complete restoration. [Balthazar Korab]

Opposite: The bold arch of the reception room fireplace repeats the curve motif and draws one to the warmth and intimacy of this secondary living room space. Wright used the same barrel chairs at his home Taliesin and at Wingspread, his house for Herbert Johnson in Wisconsin. Warm brown tones of the Roman brick blend with the golden oak and yellow, gold, and amber of the fabrics. [K. C. Kratt]

MAY HOUSE

Wright's commissions were not all as grand as the Dana and Martin houses. Most were for middle-class business people who had a sense of adventure but a more modest budget. When Grand Rapids, Michigan, clothier Meyer May and his wife, Sophie, contracted with Wright to design them a home in 1908, they were rewarded with a Prairie Style gem. In part because of the able assistance of designer George Niedecken, it was as thoroughly detailed as any of the larger residences.

Sunlight pours into the living areas through generous banks of art glass windows all across the southern facade, throwing geometric light patterns into the room (pages 42–43). The interior spaces open freely, one to another, with interesting transitions. They practically glow. The rich, golden tones—dominated by the natural color of the oak trim, floors, and furniture—are totally harmonious. Values shift easily from tan to brownish orange to tawny golds to pale yellow-greens. But there is relief from this limited palette. A bit of gray-blue sets off the carpet colors, and an uncharacteristic pink is offered in a Niedecken mural (page 39). The art glass in the windows, ceiling panels, cabinet doors, and even the fireplace mortar

joints (page 45) continue the golden theme. The mass glistens and lightens with the reflection from the windows across the room.

Squares and abstracted leaf forms are repeated in the carpet patterns, art glass, and embroidered linen patterns. Like members of a family, they all share a genetic commonality. Wright-designed furniture was supplemented in the bedrooms by Arts and Crafts pieces, especially Stickley items. The simple, sturdy shapes blend easily with the spaces and the Wright components.

Light fixtures also were specially designed to be part of the unified whole. Wall sconces like those in other Prairie Style homes are placed in banded panels throughout the main floor, but custom lamps for particular spaces also were fabricated. All use the colored art glass found in the windows. In the living room, cove lighting reflected off the ceiling provides a soft light for a harmonious room.

Within fourteen years of its construction, a large addition became the first of many changes that drastically altered the house over the years. In 1985 it was authentically restored by its new owner, Steelcase Inc. Today, it is possible to experience once again Wright's perfectly unified living environment.

Opposite: When seated in the dining room, guests could see the outdoor garden through geometric art glass on one side and a mural garden on the other side.

Left: In the master bedroom is a smaller but similar version of the golden fireplace in the living room.

Following pages: The living room furniture is more upholstered than in many of Wright's earlier homes. A slight flare at the foot of all seating and cabinet pieces, while unusual in his furniture of the period, breaks the monotony of the straight line. But the principal motif is clearly rectilinear. [Photographs by Jon Miller, © Hedrich-Blessing. Courtesy Steelcase]

LITTLE HOUSE II

Wright had already designed another home for Mr. and Mrs Francis W. Little in Peoria, Illinois, when they approached him about a new house on Lake Minnetonka in Wayzata, outside Minneapolis. Northome became one of his last Prairie Style houses when it was completed in 1914.

The living room, by far the dominant space in the house, is nearly fifty feet long. Mrs. Little was an accomplished musician and wanted the room to double as a recital space. The height of the ceiling adds to the room's grandeur. Flanked by two long walls with more than a dozen art glass windows on two levels, the room has the lightness of an outdoor pavilion. Clear glass was used in the leaded panels so that the magnificent views—the lake was to one side and the woods to the other—would not be obstructed. The delicate designs of lines and triangles, concentrated on the outer edges of the window, reach across several panels, creating a larger composition than on just the one window. The art glass skylights, an intricate checkerboard of tiny squares and triangles, are framed by heavy wood moldings.

The Littles brought some furniture from their 1903 house to their new home, and Wright augmented it with additional designs.

The rectilinear Prairie Style furniture had changed little over the decade, so that the sturdy oak shapes of tables, cabinets, and chairs adapted easily to the house's scale. The vertical spindles of the radiator covers are repeated in the base of the print table and seem to capture the rhythm of the wood marking strips across the ceiling. The strong horizontality of the entire house and the room itself pulls the scale back down to a more human level.

Foliage of the season is brought inside to fill oversized vases. *Winged Victory*, Wright's favorite classical sculpture, rises from a table top. Oriental carpets were used occasionally to add pattern to otherwise solid tones of golds and browns. Each detail contributed to the serenity of the home.

In 1972 the Little family decided to build a new house on the site. Learning that the original home would be demolished, the Metropolitan Museum of Art in New York offered to document the dismantling and purchase the parts. The living room was then rebuilt as part of the museum's American Wing. Other rooms were sold to museums and collectors. While this fragmentation is tragic and antithetical to Wright's concept of unity, it does provide an opportunity for millions of visitors to experience the interior of a Wright house.

Opposite: The living room was the grandest space in the sprawling Prairie Style house. Reconstructed in the Metropolitan Museum of Art in New York, the room's transition from a natural site to a museum setting has refocused the perception of this space as an art object. Still compelling are the linear power of the light screens, the mastery of scale and proportion, the delicate strength of the wood spindles, the subtle contrasts in color and pattern, the variety and unity within the space. Yet the original intended use of the room, as a recital space and family gathering area, prevails as the source of the room's masterful design. [Ping Amranand]

CALIFORNIA HOUSES

The 1920s were sparse years for Wright's career. His private life was chaotic, and between 1916 and 1922 he traveled back and forth to Japan, living there for long periods while supervising construction of the Imperial Hotel and a few other commissions. Despite his inattention to his practice in the United States, Wright created a group of exciting buildings in California, hoping for a while to establish a permanent office there. These California houses were inspired by the materials and spirit of the area and were built primarily of concrete.

Wright viewed concrete as an inexpensive, durable, and, most important, malleable building material without a personality of its own. His pursuit of its full potential began with Unity Temple in Oak Park, Illinois, in 1904 and continued with intermittent periods of obsession. Because concrete submits itself so willingly to whatever an architect desires, Wright sought ways to take advantage of its plasticity. The sunny California climate seemed the perfect place to do so.

After flirting with concrete ornament in the Hollyhock house in 1917, Wright designed four concrete textile block houses in the Los Angeles area between 1922 and 1926. Lloyd Wright, the architect's oldest son, actually supervised the construction of most of them after his father returned to the Midwest.

The houses recall Mayan and Japanese influences but relied heavily on American technology of the twentieth century. To create the decorative textile blocks, concrete was precast into hollow blocks on site by unskilled workers, using local rock and sand. Steel rods were then interwoven in the hollow chambers of the blocks, which were set with no mortar joints; instead, they were filled with grout or concrete to give them strength. Intended to be built inexpensively, the textile block houses proved quite the opposite. The blocks were not uniform and required tedious adaptation to lay evenly. Wright was busy in Japan and was not available to solve problems.

The geometric blocks nonetheless created striking patterns when laid up in walls. The result was cool edifices of contemporary forms, nestled into the hills overlooking Los Angeles. Their sandy texture and sculpted shapes rise like sand castles on a dune.

In Wright's Ennis house of 1923 in Los Angeles, stacked textile blocks create a colonnade through which the indoor and outdoor rooms reveal themselves. A golden Tiffany glass mosaic of wisteria glistens above the fireplace in the hallway. [Julius Shulman]

HOLLYHOCK HOUSE

High atop Hollywood's Olive Hill, Wright sculpted a home in 1917 for oil heiress and theater dévotée Aline Barnsdall. The architect responded to the barren site with a new interpretation of his organic architecture that marked the beginning of his California concrete era. Although planned for reinforced, poured concrete, it is mostly stucco on wood frame, but it still incorporates specially cast concrete ornament. The hollyhock flower, the client's favorite, was the inspiration for the abstracted decorative patterns in the concrete, art glass, and oak furniture.

Only one building of a planned performing arts complex, the house is oriented toward a center garden court and punctuated by several geometric pools. The design creates a private world where guests can freely circulate throughout the living spaces and gallery, into the gardens, and even up to the rooftop terraces for a longer view of the city.

Inside, the monochromatic, even surfaces come alive with color. The recently restored living room is another exercise in shades of gold and green. Custom oak furniture completes the inviting spaces, for which carpets also were designed. The incredibly complex, mirror-image table, lamp, and sofas that have been recreated draw guests around the central fireplace. Between the hearth and the sofas is a reflecting pool, a cooling contrast to the warm room. Over the fireplace, lattice grillework directs sunlight into the room like a theater spotlight on a star. Japanese decorative arts fit comfortably into the room, which was designed while Wright was working on the Imperial Hotel.

In 1927 Barnsdall donated the home and grounds to the city of Los Angeles, which continues to be responsible for its care and public access.

A circular pool highlights the central courtyard. Looking back at the house, a concrete passageway ornamented with stylized hollyhocks provides a compressed space that is released into the garden. The composition of geometric forms, like musical chords, creates a controlled architectural harmony. [Scot Zimmerman]

Following pages: The restoration of the living room included the recreation of the large sofa-table-lamp piece. It completes a unique setting focused on the fireplace, which is surrounded by a reflecting pool. Japanese screens are integral to the room's design and may have inspired the gold metallic paint on the walls. [© Alexander Vertikoff]

FREEMAN HOUSE

Opposite: Some of the fifty-two versions of the concrete block patterns are evident outside, massed and then balanced by the lightness of glass panels. [John Marshall]

Left: In the living room, light from the clerestory windows sheds unique patterns below. The furniture was designed by Rudolph Schindler. [John Marshall]

Following pages: The cavelike feeling inside contrasts with the vastness of the world beyond. From the living room, the city skyline stretches for miles. The power of the square motif inundates the house and is released only beyond its walls. [Julius Shulman]

The concrete house that Wright created in Los Angeles in 1923 for Samuel and Harriet Freeman is, at 1,200 square feet, a compact and pure example of his textile block system of construction. The various geometric designs cast into the blocks create a texture that dominates the feel of the building. This tactile quality gives the cool concrete material an earthy appeal.

The dominant building material is also the dominant interior design element—yet another expression of Wright's quest for unity. The geometric masses that result from stacking these sixteen-inch-square blocks express the efficient, open spaces within the home. The square is most certainly the unit of design for the building. Some of the blocks are perforated to let light filter in through the pattern; others are solid, providing a counterpoint to the texture. Some are filled with glass to create windows; others are structurally supporting. Some are grouped to create a ceiling; others are widely spaced to provide doorways. Some are stacked thirty feet high; others reach out over the hill on terrace walls.

Approaching the house, only the closed side of the second story is visible. Yet variety and imagination are apparent. Entering through a compressed hallway, the living room explodes right in front. Light, shadows, and texture are everywhere. Wright conjured up a cool, protected place out of the sun's burning rays.

The furniture, which was not designed by Wright but by a one-time Wright apprentice and friend of the Freemans, Rudolph Schindler, is as unique as the building. The versatile upholstered and cabinet pieces capture the intimacy and simplicity of the spaces; some convert to various uses. Cool concrete meets warm wood tones and golden upholstery fabrics. Pottery, native American textiles, archaeological fragments, and wooden sculptures reinforce the primitive, cavelike feeling within the home. By day, the large glass expanse draws one to the light and the city below. But at night, the fireplace in the opposite wall beckons to the protected center, a place to reflect and share ideas. It is a refuge.

For sixty years, this house was a popular gathering place for artists, actors, dancers, and musicians. In 1983 Harriet Freeman donated it to the University of Southern California, whose care and study of the building are shedding new light on Wright's novel textile block design form.

1930∫ DE∫IGN∫

The late 1920s and early 1930s were the most barren years of Wright's long career, in terms of the number of commissions. At age sixty-five, many men would have accepted this drought as a natural call to retirement. Not Wright. Never unchallenged, Wright-the-architect called on Wright-the-author and Wright-the-teacher to lead him out of financial hard times.

As a means of sorting out his life and promoting his self-proclaimed genius, Wright wrote *An Autobiography,* which was first published in 1932. This popular book, reprinted several times, inspired new interest in his work and consequently new clients. Soon afterward, he and his new wife, Olgivanna, founded the Taliesin Fellowship and began to build Taliesin West. Among the early apprentices there was Edgar J. Kaufmann, Jr., the twenty-four-year-old son of a wealthy Pittsburgh merchant. While he stayed at Taliesin for only a few months, Kaufmann, inspired by the autobiography and his experiences, introduced his father to the work of Wright, thus instigating a patronage that gave new life to the architect's career. Fallingwater, a revolutionary country house that Wright designed for the Kaufmanns, was without a doubt a powerful response to those espousing the new European International Style.

The other pivotal patron to appear in the 1930s was Herbert Johnson, president of the Johnson Wax Company. Wright's streamlined design for the firm's 1939 administration building in Racine, Wisconsin, with its lily-pad-like columns, confirmed that Wright's genius had not tired but had new energy. Wright was later asked to add a research tower to the building and design homes for Johnson and his daughter.

In these years of introspection, Wright created his two most celebrated works: Fallingwater and the Johnson Wax Administration Building. But there was plenty of time left to create his master plan for American cities, Broadacre City. The huge model, which the apprentices built, and the book and lectures he wrote about it were the subject of numerous assessments and diverse opinions. Interest blossomed in Wright's ideas. From 1935 to his death in 1959, Wright completed nearly two hundred more buildings.

At Fallingwater nooks and crannies permitted the Kaufmanns' fine sculpture collection to be dis- **played. Uncharacteristically, Wright even left some limited wall space for paintings. [Christopher Little]**

FALLINGWATER

In late 1934 Wright visited a waterfall near Mill Run, Pennsylvania, where Liliane and Edgar J. Kaufmann hoped to build a weekend retreat. Wright was moved by the beauty of its rock ledges, lush foliage, and rushing waters over Bear Run. The native vegetation, especially the rhododendron and mountain laurel, flourished in the moist shade. Sandstone boulders marked the prehistoric landscape that had been a favorite preserve for the Kaufmanns and their employees. When he received a detailed topographical map, Wright set about designing Fallingwater, which became the most renowned building of his career. Built into the side of the hill, and over—not across from—the picturesque waterfall, its design was a celebration of the site (pages 2–3). When it was completed in 1935, the Kaufmanns truly had a home where they could entertain their friends and commune with the wonders of nature. In 1963 Edgar Kaufmann, Jr., donated the house and 1,500 acres to the Western Pennsylvania Conservancy so that it would be protected and enjoyed by others.

Like a giant tree, Fallingwater grew from the site. The roots are the boulders on the valley floor. The trunk is a thirty-foot-tall layered sandstone chimney core. Its branches are low cantilevered terraces of reinforced concrete, the first-floor slab reaching eighteen feet beyond the stone piers. The rock ledges were the inspiration and became part of the composition: the four largest boulders are so integrated into the building's structure that the pivotal one is exposed in the living room as the hearth. The stream is so much a part of the house that a suspended stairway leads directly into it.

Edgar Kaufmann, Jr., described Fallingwater's relationship to the surrounding forest.

The materials of the structure blend with the colorings of the rocks and trees, while occasional accents are provided by bright furnishings, like the wildflowers or birds outside. The paths within the house, stairs and passages, meander without formality or urgency, and the house hardly has a main entrance; there are many ways in and out. Sociability and privacy are both available, as are the comforts of home and the adventures of the seasons. So people are cosseted into relaxing, into exploring the enjoyment of life refreshed in nature.

The living room, roughly 1,800 square feet of flexible space, is masterfully shaped into more intimate areas for dining and relaxing. Ceiling levels, lighting, masonry piers, and furniture groupings work together to focus attention on a certain spot, the waxed

flagstone floor stretching beneath all. Upstairs, both master and guest bedrooms open to private terraces (pages 12–13). Each has its own fireplace. The third-floor study and gallery are connected to two more terraces and a tiny treetop nook.

From the highest balcony to the plunge pool beneath the living room terrace, the diverse spaces offer opportunities for privacy or sociability. The refinements of a cultured life are accentuated by the simplicity of the natural setting. At Fallingwater, Wright's imagination and coordination set new highs.

Opposite: From the colors of the sandstone, Wright selected a light chamois for the long, graceful stretches of concrete. His favorite color, Cherokee red, outlines the long bands of windows, creating a snappy, secondary rhythm. Terraces to the east and west served as viewing platforms and gathering places.

Above: The site's key boulder became the living room hearth.

Following pages: The furniture's simple, geometric shapes provide a background for patterns and textures of handcrafted fiber arts. Red remains the principal accent to the warm buffs and grays. [Photographs by Christopher Little]

WINGSPREAD

Just north of Racine, Wisconsin, Wright orchestrated another house totally at one with its site. Only a half mile from Lake Michigan, the spot now occupied by Wingspread was once a nature preserve. It is lush with mature pines, arborvitae, wooded areas, ponds, and lagoons. The house shares thirty acres with an abundance of water-fowl and wildlife.

Wright called Wingspread another Prairie Style house, because it was similar to the zoned plans of earlier commissions such as the Coonley house of 1908. However, it is a bolder, freer inter-pretation that is quite different from its older siblings and in many ways more like a Usonian. The house was created for Herbert F. Johnson, president of the Johnson Wax Company, shortly after Wright designed the company's noted administration building. Before the house was completed in 1939, Mrs. Johnson died. Johnson moved in nonetheless and continued to live in the spacious house for twenty years. It now serves as a conference center and the home of the Johnson Foundation.

Wingspread is built on a square grid, which is incised into the highly waxed, red concrete floors, and accented with powerful diagonal lines. At the center is a monumental, curvilinear fireplace core. Around this gracefully articulated central mass are all of the living and entertaining spaces. Each has its own fireplace. Wright called this thirty-foot-high area a wigwam. Shallow steps and ceiling heights define the shift from one area of the space to another. Wings spread out in four directions like a pinwheel. One is for the master bedroom suite, one for the children's bedrooms; another is the guest wing, and the fourth is the service area.

The craftsmanship is exemplary. The only ornament is the careful handling of the building materials themselves: flawless Cherokee red brick masses; great expanses of smooth, seemingly nail-less bands of oak veneer; perfectly cut sandstone slabs; and meticulously crafted furniture.

Despite the grandeur of the spaces, the power of the hori-zontal line dominates. The wooden light decks and tiers of clerestory windows join the deeply raked horizontal mortar joints to create a visual unity. The eye is drawn to the people level. There, clusters of simple, comfortable furniture invite visitors to enjoy the variety of indoor and outdoor spaces—at the fireplace, by the pool, in the library. A few well-selected works of art complement the spaces but do not detract from their simple elegance.

Opposite: The central core is a giant curved chimney. Warm brick and oak tones are enriched by abundant natural light from above and on all sides. The curved shapes of the chimney, the stairway to an observation point, and the barrel chairs add an undulating rhythm to the primarily square space. [Rich-ard Cheek, Yale University Press]

USONIAN HOUSES

Shifts in American lifestyles and the need for economical housing challenged Wright throughout his career, particularly in the late 1930s and the 1940s when Wright observed changes in American families. Most of them owned automobiles; they were home less often; more women were working; most families had no servants; time spent in the kitchen was also family socialization time; life was more and more informal. Wright's solution was Usonian houses, a term he used to describe buildings uniquely suitable for life in the United States of North America (USONA). His concepts were a part of his larger vision for a decentralized Broadacre City.

Wright developed a pattern, a way of building, that would respond to these shifts in society. The kitchen was open to the dining area at the core of the house. Spacious living areas opened in one direction; bedrooms extended in the other direction and were small with many built-ins to conserve space. The homes usually had flat or shallow-pitched roofs and were one story. They stretched sensitively across their suburban lots, offering a private street side with few windows and an open garden side with generous terraces. Built on concrete slabs, the houses were heated by water pipes buried in the floor. Each house had a module, or unit system, that formed the basis for its construction; this unit was incised into the wet concrete floors and served as a grid on which the house was built. The square, rectangle, hexagon, and triangle took their turns as these modules.

One of the fundamental principles of Usonian architecture was that it should be affordable. Throughout his career Wright experimented with new ways of building to eliminate costly skilled craftspeople and expensive materials. He felt most challenged by clients who had big desires but a small pocketbook. He encouraged them to participate in the building themselves. Wright developed efficiencies in design that produced efficiencies in construction and lower costs, without compromising beauty— instead, reframing it. The methods were applied to small houses as well as to larger commissions and became the framework for his remaining designs.

Wright designed two houses for the Herbert Jacobses. Their first, in 1936, was his first Usonian. The second, built in Middleton, Wisconsin, in 1948, is a solar hemicycle tucked into an earthen berm on the cold north side. The curved southern wall seen here is open to solar rays that warm the house. [Ezra Stoller, © Esto]

HANNA HOUSE

Moved by Wright's philosophy of architecture, Jean and Paul Hanna, a young professor at Stanford University, approached Wright with their ideas and budget. His response was a magnificent design in Palo Alto, California, based on a hexagonal module, like a bee's honeycomb—thus giving the home its name, Honeycomb house. Wright opted for a 120-degree angle over his favored 90-degree angle, demonstrating yet another method of breaking out of boxlike rooms.

The house for Catherine and Herbert Jacobs, then under way in Madison, Wisconsin, established Wright's vision of a Usonian house. The 1936 house for the Hannas was a larger interpretation of the same concept, but its hexagonal module differed from the Jacobses' four-by-two-foot rectangle. Unfortunately, but not surprisingly for Wright, the house far exceeded the Hannas' modest budget. Somehow, it got built.

The house adapted easily to the changes in the family's needs for more than thirty-five years. During that time, they added a guest house and a hobby shop as well as a garden house. Their extensive landscaping enhanced the building's relationship to the gently sloping site. In 1974 the Hannas donated their beloved home to Stanford University. Before suffering extensive earthquake damage in 1989, it served as the home of the university's provost.

Wright's use of flexible, mostly movable, interior and exterior walls gives the home a Japanese feeling. Entire window walls swing open, allowing the living spaces to flow out onto the concrete terraces. It also permitted the couple to convert many of the spaces to new shapes and uses when the children left home. The vertical module of the redwood board-and-batten walls relates to the horizontal module. The rooms casually wrap around the contours of the site to form spaces that slowly reveal themselves. The hexagonal unit creates a natural gentleness in the meander of the spaces. The trellis-like windows frame garden views in all directions. The inner court with a cascading pool provides an embracing garden refuge.

Inside, the original furnishings repeat the hexagonal motif. Interesting patterns are created when right-angled brick joins at 120-degree angled corners. A tall fireplace reaches out of its pit and into the living room. Grass matting covers the ceiling and adds a natural texture next to the smooth wood surfaces. The home is breezy, sheltered, cool in the summer heat. Radiant-heated floors are partially covered with neutral-colored, simple-textured carpets.

In the Honeycomb house, obtuse angles seem to accept and respond to human activities more naturally than abrupt right angles. This is one of Wright's most welcoming interiors.

Following pages: The natural tones in the living room become a quiet backdrop for the exuberance of the meandering spaces. With its hexagonal module, the home has a compelling flow that carries the eye from room to room and inside to outside without interruption. These flexible, open spaces responded to the family's needs.

Opposite: The garden terrace floor continues the hexagonal module. Even the light seems to be cast in hexagonal patterns. As in Wright's other Usonian houses, terrace doors open out from the living room, inviting the patterns and colors of the magnificent garden into the house. [Photographs by Ezra Stoller, © Esto]

ROSENBAUM HOUSE

When Mildred and Stanley Rosenbaum were married in 1938, the groom's parents lured them back to Florence, Alabama, with the promise of an architect-designed home. Learning of Wright's work, the young couple eagerly sought his help. They became early pioneers of his Usonian concept of moderate-price housing for American families. Their 1,540-square-foot house, built in 1939 for $12,000, was one of Wright's finest.

Sensitively sited on two acres overlooking the Tennessee River, it is a simple horizontal statement. The cypress and brick home is based on a rectangular module and is placed on a concrete slab with heating beneath it. All walls and windows are aligned with a grid that is incised into the floor. The L-shaped plan is typically private on the street side and open at the back. Behind the entry, at the core of the house, is an open kitchen and dining area, which Wright called the workspace. One wing provides three bedrooms and two baths. The other includes an ample living room and library. A later courtyard addition, also designed by Wright, increased the bedroom area needed for the family's four sons and changed the plan to a T shape.

All rooms open freely to the outdoors through floor-to-ceiling doors and windows, borrowing space, light, and color from nature. Rows and rows of multicolored books line the walls.

Clerestory windows with perforated panels bring light into the closed side of the house. While many pieces of built-in and free-standing furniture were designed for the home using the same two-by-four-foot module, as well as the same cypress, the owners felt free to restructure the various components and to select other furniture. Charles Eames's molded plywood chairs and rectilinear upholstered pieces are compatible with the Wright tables and cabinets. Mildred Rosenbaum's favorite color, teal blue, complements the warm tones of the board-and-batten walls.

For fifty years, the home successfully responded to the changing needs of the original family. The playground became a Japanese garden. A bunk room became a weaving studio. And now the house is open to the public as a house museum.

Above: Like other Usonians, the Rosenbaum house is strongly horizontal. The front is private with few windows, but the back opens to the surrounding landscape from nearly every room. French doors welcome sunlight into the spaces. [Courtesy Rosenbaum house]

Opposite: The dining area, built into an area that is offset from the living room, opens to the kitchen on the left. Plywood chairs by Charles Eames blend naturally with the built-in cypress furniture designed by Wright. [© Carol M. Highsmith]

Opposite: Modular plywood furniture was grouped into various configurations as needed. Throughout, a neutral gray offsets the dominant Cherokee red. Cutouts in the clerestory panels, characteristic of the Usonian houses, repeat the geometric theme of the house, while they filter light and frame treetop views.

Above: A view of the modest house at dusk shows how the cypress boards have weathered to gray. Openings in the roof over the windows keep the light shining through despite the broad overhangs. The entrance porte-cochère is at right, the private terrace on the left. [Photographs by Ping Amranand]

POPE-LEIGHEY HOUSE

"Will you create a house for us? Will you?" newspaperman Loren Pope wrote to Wright in 1939.

There are certain things a man wants during life, and, of life. Material things and things of the spirit. The writer has one fervent wish that includes both. It is for a house created by you. Created is the proper word. Many another architect might be able to plan or design a house. But only you can create one that will become for us a home.

Two weeks later came the reply from Wright: "Of course I am ready to give you a house."

Simply built of cypress boards sandwiched over a plywood core, brick, and glass on a concrete pad, the house that Wright gave to Loren and Charlotte Pope in Falls Church, Virginia, eliminated all that was not essential. Another of Wright's L-shaped Usonian plans, built around a large tulip poplar tree, the 1941 house was a modest 1,200 square feet. Its flexibility meant that less space was needed. The ornament came from the materials themselves: the placement of windows, wood joinery and cutouts, patterns of the masonry. Simple linen and jute mats in a biscuit color covered the red floors.

The living and dining areas are a few steps down from the entry level, so that the changing planes define activities, create interest, and adapt the building to its site. A sanctum or study is to the right of the entry. Opening to the outside on two sides, the house is filled with light and changing shadows all day. Despite the simplicity of the economical two-bedroom home, it is visually stimulating in every direction. The component seating and table groups can be gathered into various compositions for dining, conversation, lounging, or bridge parties. Again, Wright designed for efficiency and flexibility as well as aesthetics. One naturally followed the other.

The Popes sold their house to Marjorie and Robert Leighey in 1946. After living there for eighteen years, the Leigheys learned that a planned interstate highway was destined to go right through their living room. Rather than see it demolished, Marjorie Leighey donated the house to the National Trust for Historic Preservation. It was then dismantled, relocated, and rebuilt on the grounds of another National Trust property, the early nineteenth-century Woodlawn Plantation, in Mount Vernon, Virginia—a study in residential contrasts. While house moving is not the best way to save a building, it may, in some cases, be the only way.

WALTER HOUSE

After selling his road-building company in 1944, Lowell Walter sought to build a retirement home. Rather than move to Florida or California, he selected a site on a family farm in Quasqueton, Iowa, where his family had lived for generations. Walter wanted an architect who would be sensitive to the beauties of the Midwest. What Wright produced the following year was a complex of buildings, including the house, a two-story river pavilion, and an outdoor hearth called "council fires," all suited to the informal lifestyle of the countryside. The eleven-acre site is now operated by the Iowa Department of Natural Resources, to which Walter bequeathed it in 1981.

One enters the estate through Wright-designed iron gates, down a drive lined with evergreens of many varieties, including local cedars. Only low shrubberies were planted near the house itself, creating a soft mat for its base. Gradually, the house, called Cedar Rock, is approached across a terrace, past flower planters. Sited on a hill overlooking a bend in the Wapsipinicon River, the house is built of red brick and based on a square five-foot, three-inch module. Massive masonry walls lift the home above the hillside, create delicate grilles, and define indoor and outdoor spaces. The roof is reinforced concrete, cantilevering out beyond the walls but pierced over the windows.

The living room, or garden room, is actually a rotated square projecting out from the bedroom wing like a flower on a stem. Waxed walnut boards run the length of the gallery and are used in the shelves, defining the room's shape. Pieces of the beautifully crafted walnut furniture can be fitted together in various arrangements. The curved edges, either concave or convex, like that of the wood moldings, repeat the curve of the roof edge. A fireplace, large enough to accommodate five-foot logs, rises from its shallow pit. Tropical plants hang from planters above the soffit and fill planters built into the red concrete floor. The ceiling is pierced with square skylights to nourish the interior gardens. The walls are glass on three sides, mitered at the corners, and mirrored on the fourth. The room is an open garden pavilion with only a roof for shelter.

The living room overlooks the ambling Wapsipinicon River. Generous windows and a pierced roof flood the room with enough light for an interior garden. Smooth lines in the fine walnut cabinetry create elegance in this country setting. [Ezra Stoller, © Esto]

ZIMMERMAN HOUSE

Dr. Isadore Zimmerman and his wife, Lucille, a nurse, were one of many of Wright's clients who were drawn to his work through his autobiography. They were delighted with the opportunity to let Wright transform their personal interests and lifestyle into a concrete statement that suited their site. In that they allowed Wright a free rein and also shared his love of music, they were ideal clients. Isadore Zimmerman was an accomplished violinist who also studied and played the piano, and Lucille played the piano and cello.

While considered a Usonian design because of its chronological age and construction style, the Zimmerman house, built in Manchester, New Hampshire, in 1950, recalls Wright's earlier Prairie Style period as well. Its concept was economical, but the execution was more extravagant because of the selection of materials and the owners' demand for first-class craftsmanship.

The broad, sheltering, gently sloped roof and horizontal profile nestle the home quietly into its wooded lot. Although Wright specified wood shingles, red clay tiles were ultimately used on the roof but have since been replaced with asphalt. The street elevation is private, with only a strip of special perforated concrete blocks framing small windows above the red brick base. This combination of materials was new for Wright. Specially beveled, carefully selected cypress boards were screwed into place, then the hole was plugged, making it invisible. A four-foot-square grid was incised into the concrete floor, but the vertical unit used throughout the house was thirteen inches.

The garden room, the main living area, doubled as a concert space for the Zimmermans' friends, who gathered to share their love of music. The quartet stand is based on the one used at Taliesin. The southwest exposure opens to a beautifully landscaped garden abundant with rhododendron and punctuated with oak, pine, ash, and maple trees. Golden light fills the space on cold winter evenings. Five brick piers, with glass between, create a structural rhythm. Planters extend from one side of the glass to the other, blurring the distinction between inside and out. The other rooms are small to accommodate the generous living room within the limits of the 1,458 square feet of the entire house.

A high-back bench, chairs, and hassocks are upholstered in handwoven fabrics, selected by Wright, in golds and rusts. A six-panel Japanese screen is attached to the end wall. Lamps have Japanese paper inserts. Over the years, the Zimmermans became avid art collectors. While they could not display paintings, their home became a personal gallery for their collection of three-dimensional art. They were especially fond of the pottery of Edwin Scheier but also collected sculpture by others.

Consequently, they developed a close relationship with the Currier Gallery of Art. On Lucille Zimmerman's death in 1988, her home was bequeathed to the gallery, which has undertaken its restoration and provides guided tours.

Above: The living room gains its perceived size by annexing the adjoining terrace. Planters line the glass, which seems to dissolve the definition between inside and outside just as the mitered corner window does. The private wooded site became a part of daily life within the home. [Photographs by Ezra Stoller, © Esto]

Opposite: The garden room seems spacious despite the house's modest size. Behind the brick fireplace are the workspace and the bedrooms. Scored with the module of the house, the waxed, red concrete floor covers radiant heating coils. The furniture is economical and flexible as well as a freestanding architectural element.

LIVING WITH WRIGHT

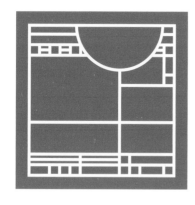

LIVING WITH WRIGHT'S EXTRAORDINARILY INTEGRATED VISION OF WHAT A HOUSE SHOULD BE POSES REAL CHALLENGES. WHAT CAN CHANGE? WHAT SHOULD STAY THE SAME? MANY PRIVATE OWNERS HAVE MET THIS CHALLENGE WITH RESPECT—AND SOME PATIENCE.

Opposite: Mary and William Palmer have successfully faced the challenges of living in their Wright home in Ann Arbor, Michigan, for forty years. Fortunately, their personal interests in gardening, Japanese culture, and music are in sympathy with their exquisite Usonian house. The waxed red floor, incised with a triangular module like the house itself, serves as a glowing backdrop for the autumnal colors of the living area. The room is a large triangle that projects into a woodland garden that the Palmers have created and nurtured for many years, embracing the Wrightian spirit with which their house was designed in 1952. [Balthazar Korab]

THE CHALLENGE

The vast majority of Wright's residences, 269, are still privately owned by individuals or families. They are not museums. They are lived in by people who may have growing children, or hobbies, or pets. And living in a house designed by a world-renowned architect presents some difficult choices when one wants to update or adapt to new life patterns. The inherent public responsibility of owning such a house is, one hopes, repaid by the daily rewards of living in the harmonious environments that Wright created.

Reflected Marjorie Leighey about the Pope-Leighey house:

At first there is quiet pleasure and thankfulness for being surrounded by something so admirable to look upon. Then comes the business of living. . . . Comes a time of rebellion, an anger at any dwelling-place that presumes to dictate how its occupants live. . . . Comes the time for decision. Do we truly like the house? Would we rather live here than anywhere else? Again the beauty spoke. . . . Intelligence was put to work to see how to live within the now-accepted limitations.

Private owners like Marjorie Leighey, especially those who are not the original clients, have had to determine how their homes can best respond to their needs and their tastes and yet not upset the integrity of Wright's masterful spaces. Some have indiscriminately altered their buildings, tragically ignoring the original design intent and leaving great challenges for future preservationists. Others have carefully and sensitively made alterations. Some of these changes have been restorations, reversing inappropriate renovations.

Still other homeowners have not made architectural changes but have, for one reason or another, furnished their homes, at least partially, with items that were not specifically designed for them but that are perfectly compatible. These owners have been able to respond to the powerful expectations of Wright's legacy without sacrificing their own individuality. In fact, each is enhanced.

The owners of the homes shown here are representative of many who have successfully personalized their Wright houses. They have often gone to extraordinary lengths to do so and are to be commended for their investment in America's architectural heritage.

The current owners of the Henderson house have carefully furnished their early Prairie house with appropriate period items. The print table in the entrance hall is like ones on which Wright displayed his favorite Japanese woodblock prints. [© Judith Bromley]

HENDERSON HOUSE

One of the earliest Prairie Style designs, the F. B. Henderson home in Elmhurst, Illinois, is often compared to the Hickox house built the previous year, 1900, in Kankakee. The similar floor plans include an elongated octagon that is shared by the living room, dining room, and library. The hipped roof and ribbons of art glass windows beneath broad sheltering eaves clearly reflect Wright's style of the decade. The space flows freely through the house, which is anchored by a broad, central chimney. The subtle design of the brickwork gives an illusion of a concave arch over the hearth, drawing one to the center.

The current owners compare their home to a city loft space because of the openness of the first floor. A myriad of white and clear windows in simple compositions of squares and rectangles further extend the rooms into the garden and adjoining veranda. Original colors have been returned to the walls. The characteristic autumnal scheme has pumpkin walls below, with a stippled, light maize color above the russet-stained birch wood banding.

Lacking information about the original furnishings, the family has sought reproductions of other Prairie Style and Arts and Crafts furniture. Some are custom designs; others were mass-produced. They blend smoothly and compatibly with the architecture of the rooms. The caramel leather seat covering of the settle, which is a reproduction of a Wright design for the Greene house in Aurora, Illinois, draws its color from the brick. A Stickley rocker echoes the rectilinear forms. The oak dining room furniture, recently custom made, was inspired by similar designs for the William Martin house in Oak Park and the Barton house in Buffalo. The octagonal posts of the chairs and table base repeat the octagonal bay in which they rest. Beneath, Oriental and Turkish carpets in geometric designs tie together groupings of furniture within the larger spaces.

When family members turned their attention to renovating the landscape, they sought to complement the rigidity of the house's geometry with a natural, prairie garden. The undulating curves of the garden beds lead to protected play areas and quiet places to rest. Perennials, trees, and shrubs, particularly ones native to the midwestern prairie, were selected to provide a continuously changing display of colors and textures throughout the seasons. The bone stucco walls, trimmed with brown and capped with a cedar-shingled roof, provide a neutral background for the magnificent natural forms from which the house was born.

BOYNTON HOUSE

It is curious that a house built for a widower and his teenage daughter would have such generous dining and kitchen facilities. A cook and a maid also lived in the home, but it is not known if the businessman, Edward E. Boynton, or in future years his married daughter, were avid entertainers. Wright beautifully articulated and carefully supervised the construction in 1908 of this classic Prairie Style home in Rochester, New York. So, it is assumed that the attention he paid to the food preparation and serving areas was a reflection of the client's interest.

The spacious dining room has two tables. The larger one has low lamp columns near each corner that also serve as flower holders. Not as high or obtrusive as those on the tables of the Robie or May houses, they focus the diners' attention on the intimacy of the table gathering. The smaller table near the expansive window bay overlooks the garden and would have been perfect for the two Boyntons dining alone. The room is further highlighted by art glass–covered ceiling lights and a band of clerestory windows over the light screen on the south wall. The dominant motif in the plentiful art glass is the square.

The kitchen retains the original, simple pine cabinets, which have been restored by the current owners. A wood-color laminate now covers the counter tops, replacing the original wood, but the center island is still topped with hard maple. A commercial range and a restaurant rack above the island are practical additions. The maple floor, covered with linoleum by a previous owner, has been restored. Storage space is augmented by an adjoining pantry, now a gallery for the owners' handmade pottery collection, as well as a huge basement pantry. Baskets and other pieces of favorite art collected at art fairs around the country add to the personality of the home.

The two principal bedroom suites clearly respond to the desires of the two original occupants. The master suite has simple built-in cabinets but minimal closets in the dressing room. It is spacious yet simply appointed, perfect for a man. Young Beulah's rooms, on the other hand, have generous closets and built-in cabinets in the dressing room, ample space for many dresses and gowns. Mirrors around the dressing table fold open for a complete viewing.

The care and spirit with which the Boynton house was built are matched by the attention of the conscientious current owners.

Above: The pantry provided storage and a preparation area for this home designed for entertaining. The new owners' pottery collection and Oriental carpet add unusual interest to what was once just a simple serving area.

Opposite: The kitchen of the Boynton house is essentially original. Only small modifications have been made to update the turn-of-the-century room. The oak cabinets and the center island have new laminate tops, and a restaurant rack has been added for storage. Track lighting focuses light on various work spaces.

Following pages: The expansive dining room is a spectacular stage for entertaining. The larger of two tables is beneath a low ceiling and framed art glass lights. Clerestory panels shed light onto the table, which has its own built-in light columns. The other table, in a higher space within an elaborate art glass bay, is surrounded by the garden view. A linear band wraps around the entire room to provide the needed human scale for an intimate gathering. The owners' art and carpet collection complements the simplicity of the three-dimensional geometric forms. New wall sconces maintain the square detail of the room. [Photographs by Andy Olenick, Fotowerks]

INGALLS HOUSE

The projecting porch, cantilevered balconies, and simple, stucco surfaces of this 1909 house in River Forest, Illinois, are reminiscent of the house Wright designed for Elizabeth Gale in Oak Park the same year. However, the symmetry and formality of the street facade are somewhat unusual for Wright. Even the art glass window designs are symmetrical, a bow of triangles above a rectangle with a low hipped roof like the house's own profile. Resting far back on its generous suburban lot, the house appears tranquil.

First-floor spaces radiate from a central Roman brick fireplace, with smooth oak moldings linking and defining the various planes. Upstairs, four bedrooms and one bathroom surround the central hall. It was a simple but compact plan that fulfilled the desire of the clients, Mr. and Mrs. J. Kibben Ingalls, for maximum ventilation.

But the present owners wished to stretch out and increase their living area as their family needs grew. The tiny, outdated kitchen was a particular concern. Inspired by Wright's own symmetry, they saw an opportunity to expand the home without altering the primary spaces or the street facade. They nearly mirrored the east elevation on the west side. Additions to Wright's buildings, usually discouraged, require courage as well as a total understanding of and respect for the original design intention. The result here is a unified plan that enhances rather than diminishes the house's harmony.

The original kitchen and a 1926 porch addition by Wright apprentice William Drummond were removed, and a large, modern kitchen–family room was added. Matching Wright's plan for the front of the house, the back includes a terrace with a cantilevered roof. A bit more width was achieved by making the north and south bays added on the west slightly larger than those on the east . The new informal cooking and gathering space nearly doubles in size in warmer months when activities reach out onto the terrace overlooking the garden. Upstairs, a small bedroom was enlarged, and a ribbon of windows replaced the single original one. In total, twenty-one new art glass windows and doors were fabricated to match the originals.

All of the changes were carefully documented, leaving a complete historical record. Every detail, every molding, every finish, and, most important, the scale and open plan are in keeping with Wright's grammar for the house.

Opposite top: The addition to the back of the house mirrors the front elevation and repeats all of the elements so sensitively that the home, while altered, is enhanced—a challenge for any owner of a historic house. The deck extends beyond the enlarged kitchen area and adds additional space in warm weather.

Opposite bottom: A spacious new kitchen replaced a tiny outdated one. Appliances are hidden behind oak doors, including a slatted screen for the microwave. Moldings continue detailing used throughout the house, maintaining the flow of space. Dinner is served on a china design from Wright's Imperial Hotel. [Photographs © Steve Grubman]

COONLEY PLAYHOUSE

When their glorious, pavilioned estate, the Coonley house, was completed in 1908, Mr. and Mrs. Avery Coonley were so energized that they decided to build a school in Riverside, Illinois, to further their ideals of progressive education. In 1912 Wright produced a cubist composition reminiscent of a Froebel block construction from his childhood. Dozens of colorful art glass windows, inspired by the balloons, flags, and confetti of parades, lined the walls. Their bright primary colors and lively geometric designs make them some of Wright's most famous windows. Sadly, the building served as a primary school only for a few years. Over the next sixty years, it was remodeled extensively, and most of the windows were sold.

Energetic new owners have thoughtfully restored the Coonley playhouse, including meticulously reproducing most of the windows using photographs and existing examples as their guide. While the open plan serves their needs as a home, it is also a splendid gallery space for their extraordinary collection of decorative arts. Fused glass is displayed in and on Arts and Crafts cabinets, illuminated by light from the three tall front windows. Ribbons of clerestory windows allow treetop views but no distractions.

In the other direction, one is drawn to the fireplace, three steps up on a stage. Nearby, chairs and tables designed by noted furniture designer George Nakashima work as components much like Wright's Usonian furniture. They can be regrouped easily for different purposes. All are constructed of walnut to match the extensive millwork in the room. Handwoven fabrics, some with colorful, geometric designs inspired by the windows and subtle grillework patterns, cover the seat cushions and stools.

Following pages: To avoid blocking the view of the hearth yet provide seating there, the owners commissioned Nakashima to create a piece that would solve this dilemma and match chairs of his they already owned. The Roman brick and plaster walls provide a neutral background for sculpture and other art. [Chester Brummel]

Recapturing the original schoolroom feeling of the front of the house, the owners have surrounded not just one but several Stickley tables with chairs. While these serve as pedestals for artworks, they also function as work or dining tables, perfect for large dinner parties. [© Judith Bromley]

BOGK HOUSE

Born in 1916 while Wright was immersed in the construction of the Imperial Hotel, this town house in Milwaukee was an artistic amalgam of various inspirational sources. It was built for the family of F. C. Bogk, a civic leader and banker. Whether seen as a transitional design or as a unique statement of its own, the house is unquestionably successful. A low hipped roof shelters the richly ornamented brick cube. Like a treasure box, it holds many jewels.

The living room, one and a half stories high, bestows its magical gifts. Originally painted metallic gold with a celadon-colored ceiling, it has a distinct Oriental flavor. Fortunately, the clients shared Wright's fascination with Japanese art. George Niedecken, Wright's able associate in Milwaukee, coordinated the interiors. Small squares of golden glass sparkle in the windows. More small squares march around the edges of the cabinetry, adding to the rhythm. Multiple custom carpets with medallions composed of squares in a variety of sizes and colors were designed to unify the spaces and confirm the color scheme. Attached and free-standing furniture expresses the grammar of the Prairie School but has a subtle Japanese feeling.

Walnut moldings wrap the walls, leading the eye from one interesting space to the next. Passing a fish pond, one is drawn up three stairs, beyond a planter with lanterns in a garden alcove, to the dining room. A wall of vertical art glass windows opens the room to the garden. At the center is another version of Wright's well-known straight-back chairs and rectangular table. These pieces, however, are partially caned, a unique and possibly Japanese variation. Custom light fixtures and a buffet complete the unified environment.

In the early 1960s the current owners commissioned Wright's followers at Taliesin to refresh the home's interiors. The soft earthen color scheme was changed to jewel tones of turquoise, carnelian, and citron. Carpets were rewoven in the original patterns but in the new colors; the originals were given to a museum. Furniture that remained has been augmented with pieces Wright designed for the Heritage-Henredon Furniture Company in the 1950s and with others designed by the Taliesin architects. New upholstery fabrics were selected. The house became a brighter version of its former self.

Vertical lighting fixtures are recessed into the walls, offering diffused light through art glass panels and repeating the verticality of the tall windows and masonry piers. [Eric Oxendorf]

STORER HOUSE

John Storer's 1923 house in Hollywood became the manifestation of Wright's newest synthesis of experiences and influences—a textile block house. Built for a retired doctor, the house encountered innumerable problems during construction, as did the other textile block houses. The cost overruns were enormous. Sadly, Storer died, bankrupt, in 1927. His dream home passed from hand to hand until 1984, when it was purchased by a film producer, who has now completed a comprehensive restoration enhanced by his own collections.

In a most unusual plan, two bedrooms are on the first floor, and others are above them on the main floor along with the dining room and kitchen, which open onto garden terraces. The living room rests immediately above the dining room, on the top floor, like a watch tower, with verandas for scanning vistas. Columns of glass and textile blocks rise two stories on both sides of the living-dining core.

Four geometric block designs are rhythmically intermixed in vertical and horizontal patterns, forming solid walls, windows, grilles, fireplaces, terraces, and pools. They sculpt imaginative and mysterious indoor and outdoor rooms from the earth.

The home is furnished with an extraordinary collection of Wright and Arts and Crafts decorative objects. Because no furniture was custom designed, the owner has blended pieces made for other Wright buildings: a Prairie Style chair comfortably shares space with a Usonian chair, related by their rectilinear origins. Designed in the center of Wright's career, the house seems to serve as a bridge between his various furniture styles now seen within its walls.

While generally faithful to the original plan, the owner and his architect, Eric Lloyd Wright, grandson of Wright, made two sensitive changes. They added a swimming pool, edged in matching textile blocks, that fits neatly into the back of the tight hillside lot. A modern kitchen also was installed without disturbing the historic architecture but deriving its forms and inspiration from it.

Following pages: The living room now doubles as a retrospective exhibition of Wright's designs, supplemented with other compatible classic works. [Oberto Gili, *House & Garden.* © 1990]

Textile blocks line the entrance terrace, with its refreshing pool. The house's landscaping, designed by Wright's son Lloyd, softens the edges of the blocks and naturally emphasizes various elements. [© Yukio Futagawa]

AULDBRASS

Wright was soon given an opportunity to apply his Usonian concepts to a southern plantation. The result was a rambling, informal complex of residential and farm buildings in Yemassee, South Carolina, that was far from the formality of the traditional southern mansion. The Leigh Stevens family occupied Auldbrass plantation beginning in 1939 and owned the home for more than thirty years.

Based on a hexagonal module, thirty inches on a side, the spaces take on an undulating openness. Wright reacted to the ubiquitous live oak trees and the sway of the Spanish moss by adopting their angle for the house's walls. All of the walls thus are sloped inward nine degrees, as well as from left to right—certainly creating a complex composition of angles to challenge the masons and carpenters. An abstracted version of moss is the basis for the downspout designs that fall from the corners. The pattern in the glass doors recalls a live oak branch. Tidewater cypress planks form the walls around the radiant-heated Cherokee red slab floor. Overhead, 33,000 square feet of new pleated copper roof shelters all.

As in antebellum days, the kitchen was placed in a separate building connected to the main house by an open pergola, which isolated the cooking heat; the connecting space has now been enclosed, creating a long dining room between the areas. A modular table of three five-foot hexagons, two parallelograms, and three triangles can be arranged in a variety of patterns suitable for up to eighteen guests. A breakfast room overlooks the pool. Cool breezes are invited in through dozens of french doors opening to terraces on all sides.

The complexity of this angular puzzle continues. Perforated screens above are cut in diagonal patterns inspired by the Yemassee Indians, creating a shadow stencil for the light. Only a few pieces of the cypress plywood furniture that Wright designed still remain in the home. They have been restored, and dozens of new pieces were constructed from original designs, all of which are based on a hexagonal unit. Triangular hassocks (partial hexagons) are clustered in various patterns; benches, shelving, and counter tops wrap around hexagonal walls; chair legs angle out beyond chair backs; hexagonal beds have adjoining triangular tables. Textured upholstery fabrics and soft blue-greens complement the warm tones of the wood, brick, leather, and colored floor. Despite the complexity, the abiding feeling is tranquility.

Wright was called back to make modifications in 1951, but the years that followed took their toll on the property. In 1987 it was rescued by a new owner, who has worked diligently to recapture the original spirit. Since then, all of the buildings, furnishings, and grounds have been meticulously restored. Auldbrass is again a collector's hospitable retreat that provides an alternative to our right-angled world.

Opposite top: The complex composition of angles in the house begins with the nine-degree inward slope of the walls, which mirrors the slant of the surrounding live oak trees. Numerous 60- and 120-degree angles are created by the hexagonal module on which the house is built.

Opposite bottom: The dining area was created from the passageway between the kitchen and the main house. Various component tables and chairs are clustered to take advantage of the view of the pool and the garden. The setting is informal and relaxed and at one with the site.

Following pages: Carefully selected accessories enrich the living area. Stuffed wild animals, watching from walls and ledges, pay homage to Auldbrass's years of service as a hunting lodge. Angular Arts and Crafts lamps, ceramics, and copper carry on the theme. [Photographs © Yukio Futagawa]

BROWN HOUSE

In designs for several cooperative residential subdivisions, Wright combined his interest in affordable housing with his ideas for community planning. One such project was the 1947 plan for Parkwyn Village in Kalamazoo, Michigan, which laid out dozens of circular lots around a small lake. The common area between the circles was planted with native vegetation.

In 1949 Eric and Ann Brown built one of four Wright-designed homes that were completed on a gracefully flowing street. Like the others, it was constructed of specially designed blocks of cast concrete, a readily available and economical material in the postwar era. Using a square module, the house extended 135 feet to include five bedrooms for the couple's three children, father-in-law, and housekeeper, but it still maintained the intended benefits of simplicity. The shallow-pitched roof with a fine gravel cover nearly blends into the gravel driveway, presenting a sheltering entrance.

The fireplace—with its surrounding pool, a dramatic feature of the spacious living room—has a six-foot-wide opening to accommodate extra-large logs. All rooms but one face the southwest to maximize the sun's warmth in this northern climate. A complementary color scheme arose from the architect's desire to use gold and the client's fondness for blue-green. Brightly colored pillows, nubby textured fabrics, and ceilings of Honduran mahogany bring additional warmth into the cool gray rooms.

For four decades the home has successfully adapted to the changing needs of the family. Ann Brown's interest in the arts was considered in the early plans and continues to be served by the spaces. The living room converts to a concert hall when the two pianos are surrounded by the numerous modular seating pieces. The fine acoustics needed for her piano classes also manage to protect the bedrooms from excessive noise. The children's bunk room has recently become her painting studio. And the desire for space in which to exhibit her work and their collection of paintings found a creative solution: wide shelves were placed along one of the few plain walls, and paintings are stacked several deep on each. Those visible on top are rotated to provide a personal gallery with any number of changing exhibitions.

The simple, neutral concrete surfaces serve as a canvas for the family, their activities, and their art.

Opposite: One of the challenges of living in a Wright house is finding wall space for paintings. Ann Brown devised a set of shelves near the entrance to hold her collection of paintings. Those on top are changed whenever desired. With its surrounding pool, the fireplace is the focus of the living room. [Balthazar Korab]

LOVNESS STUDIO

In his Usonian period, Wright was particularly challenged by prospective clients who approached him with overwhelming enthusiasm but a small budget. Such was the case with Donald and Virginia Lovness of Stillwater, Minnesota. Wright encouraged them to undertake a "do-it-yourself" house to save money, as he did with many other clients in the postwar years.

The house that had been estimated at $83,000 cost them only $20,000 in 1955—plus, of course, a treasury of personal commitment and two years of back-breaking effort. Originally conceived as a Usonian Automatic, Wright's experimental system using specially cast concrete blocks, the design evolved into a stone structure at the owners' insistence. Stone by stone, the young Lovnesses built their home according to Wright's design.

What they call their studio is a compact plan based on a simple four-foot-square module. Dolomite masonry piers support a cantilevered flat roof above a concrete slab floor. The open side of the house has floor-to-ceiling doors and windows, mitered at the corners, welcoming nature inside. Light is drawn into the house's closed side through square clerestory windows in the workspace. The geometric elements overlap and interrelate with each other and with the stone columns and decks of the building itself, creating a multidimensional sculpture. Donald Lovness, an accomplished woodworker, has continued to build, including numerous pieces of oak furniture designed by Wright for their home; Virginia Lovness does the finishing and upholstery. Together, architect and clients created a home with the richness and serenity of a temple.

Situated on a wooded hill above a small semiprivate lake, the house is a restful, artful retreat. Its low profile, not visible from the street, emerges at the end of a narrow drive with a pond on one side and a lake on the other. The 26,000 pine trees planted on the former pasture land have matured into a surrounding forest.

In 1972, after four years of work, one of four cottages that Wright designed for their lakefront was completed. Nestled into its lot, the cottage contributes to the harmony of the setting, repeating many of the house's elements and sharing the beauty of the site.

The Lovnesses built more furniture for their three-level cottage, including a table and chairs in the dining area based on other Wright furniture designs. [Photographs © Norman McGrath]

The house's dining table and chairs, built by the owners, create a rhythmic composition as they unite with the shelving unit that separates the workspace from the dining area. A layered light fixture of squares and rectangles is suspended above. Red is again used as an accent to the natural tones of the wood and stone.

The Lovness studio has a simple plan yet an elegance that stems from the spirit of the architect-client relationship. The personal interests of the owners are reflected here—their meticulous woodworking and passion for Asian art are at one with the simplicity of the architecture.

PALMER HOUSE

Wright often attracted clients who shared his interests as much as they liked his architecture. They hoped that their home would be more than a shelter from the elements, just a place to sleep and eat—that it would be a life-enriching environment. They were rewarded with homes that nourished their interests and their spirits.

When Mary Palmer, a graduate in music theory, visited her first Wright home, she later wrote, "His architecture is like a Beethoven quartet. It is vibrant. It is exciting. It is harmonious." She related to Wright's ability to compose a building. Together, Mary and William Palmer worked with Wright to create a new opus that has become more beautiful every year.

A triangular module was the basis for their home in Ann Arbor, which was built in 1952 on a protected hillside near the University of Michigan, where William Palmer taught economics. Entering from the carport, one gradually ascends a dozen broad, shallow stairs in a long, open corridor of russet brick with bands of perforated ceramic blocks, their pattern reflecting the house's floor plan. To the left, toward the light, the space of the living area bursts forth. Straight ahead, a narrow passageway leads to the bedroom wing, located in a second triangle.

The primary room is a large triangle that projects dramatically into a meticulously landscaped garden. Clear-grained, red tidewater cypress boards rise to the ceiling above. Ambers, mossy greens, and rusts, inspired by the tones of the cypress boards, have been used for upholstery fabrics and cushions. Handwoven throws, scarves, and Japanese textiles add counterpoints. A delicate pattern covers, then hangs, like an obi, from the backs of the dining chairs, softening the edges of the cypress. Down several shallow stairs, broad eaves provide shelter to the terrace, an extension of the indoor space.

The Palmers' interest in gardening and Japanese culture intensified in their new home. Japanese floral arrangements inside lead the eye beyond, to a garden that has been gradually, naturally, evolving for four decades.

In the living room, triangles and parallelograms form as the furniture and house merge. By day, the waxed red floor reflects light from the windows. At night, indirect lighting in decks casts a golden glow as it reflects off the cypress ceiling. [Balthazar Korab]

Opposite: The Palmers were moved by restful pauses in the temple gardens they visited in Japan and sought to establish that experience in their own garden. Working with former Wright associate John Howe, in 1964 they built a triangular garden house that repeats the module and style of the main house. [Balthazar Korab]

Above: While the house looks outward, the garden house in the Palmers' hillside looks inward, a deliberate spiritual metaphor. Simple Japanese floral arrangements focus attention on particular architectural details in this intimate, sunken, and carefully controlled space. The garden itself was developed by the Palmers to reflect

Wrightian principles. To the original white pine and hardwoods have been added more pines, English yews, holly, leucothoe, ferns, bleeding hearts, and a profusion of euonymous. Thousands of bulbs begin each season's pageantry. Native woodland flowers are clustered along the shady, bark-covered paths that meander along the hill-

side. An informal water course with a pool reflects and cools as it moves the eye through the garden. The garden house is a destination in itself or a stop during a walk along the garden path. [© Judith Bromley]

THE WRIGHT INFLUENCE

WRIGHT INSPIRED SEVERAL GENERATIONS OF ARCHITECTS. FOR SEVENTY YEARS, HE TAUGHT ORGANIC ARCHITECTURE, AND YOUNG ARCHITECTS LISTENED. THOSE COMMITTED TO HIS DEEPLY HELD PRINCIPLES CONTINUE TO RESIST FASHIONS AND PROVIDE UNIQUE AMERICAN DESIGNS.

Opposite: The Fisher house in Sisters, Oregon, designed by former Wright apprentice Milton Stricker, was created a century after Wright designed his first home in Oak Park and is located 2,000 miles away. Yet the principles underlying each are the same. The house created for the Fishers is a reflection of the uniqueness of the occupants; it embraces its site; it uses natural materials, some taken from the surrounding area; it is centered on a warming hearth; it draws its colors from a natural palette. It is a unity of color and form. [Randy Shelton, Architectural Images]

WRIGHT'S ASSOCIATES

Frank Lloyd Wright's contribution to American architecture did not end with his death in 1959. It is alive and well. He directly inspired hundreds of apprentices who worked at his side in his Oak Park studio and, later, at the two Taliesins. The Taliesin Fellowship, which began accepting students in 1932, provided a hands-on apprenticeship in designing, building, and artful living. Some stayed for only a few weeks, others for decades, a few for a lifetime. Many carried Wright's principles with them as they established their own practices and developed their own admirers. With Taliesin Architects, Ltd., a for-profit subsidiary of the Frank Lloyd Wright Foundation, the fellowship continues to teach through practical experience.

Wright taught principles, not a style to be slavishly imitated. The degree to which the former associates have individualized their interpretation of those principles of organic architecture varies greatly. Some of the early draftsmen in the Oak Park studio deviated little from Wright's actual Prairie Style designs. In fact, their buildings are often mistaken for his. Wright depended on his architects to be extensions of his hand—as he was a "pencil" in Louis Sullivan's hand—to produce thousands of drawings and make on-site decisions. This expectation of fidelity became a privilege and a burden.

In contrast, some who studied with Wright in the later years at Taliesin, such as John Lautner, have strongly resisted being categorized as practicing a Wright style, despite Wright's profound impact. "Architecture in its truest sense," said Lautner, "may not be academically defined. If it is, it becomes a dead, non-growing entity or cliché." The majority of the former apprentices still practicing today would no doubt agree. Countless other architects never worked in Wright's studio but had parallel careers or studied his work thoughtfully from afar. It would be futile to estimate the impact of this one man on the architecture profession during the past century—as well as on all of us whose perceptions of architecture have been irrevocably changed.

The houses that follow are a small sample of the work of some of those whose response to the needs of their clients was based on their experience with Frank Lloyd Wright.

Wright with his Taliesin Fellowship in 1937. In the top row, the second, third, and fourth from the left are John Lautner, John Howe, and Gene Masselink. In the bottom row, second from right, is Wesley Peters. [Hedrich-Blessing, Chicago Historical Society]

BARR HOUSE

During the twelve active years of Wright's Oak Park studio, some two dozen draftsmen and one woman moved in and out through its doors. Many came for only a few weeks to work on a project; others were more steady assistants. Among the latter was William Drummond, who came to Wright in 1899 and stayed for most of the next decade. On leaving Wright's studio, not long before Wright himself left to go to Europe in 1909, Drummond established himself as a less troublesome alternative to Wright. Many opportunities came his way from past and potential Wright clients, Mrs. Avery Coonley among them. He was particularly well received in River Forest, where he completed sixteen commissions, including his own home next door to his coworker Isabel Roberts.

This stucco, board-and-batten house designed for librarian Charles Barr in River Forest in 1912 was a typical commission. Although it was prepared during his three-year partnership with Louis Guenzel, it is distinctly from Drummond's hand. The indirect side entrance is gracefully sheltered and defined by the landscaping and a small projecting wall. The crisp, clean-edged lines and angles are characteristic of his version of the Prairie Style. The horizontal emphasis in the bands of art glass windows, shallow hipped roof, wide overhangs, and simple geometric forms are similar to those from Wright's office. Drummond was adept at the grammar of the Prairie Style, borrowing from Wright without actually copying him.

The differences are most apparent inside. A bold fireplace mass anchors the house at its center and opens on three sides to the living room, dining room, and hallway. The living room gives way to a projecting front porch and adjoins the dining room in a compact but seemingly spacious plan. The simple lines and neutral color of the owners' furniture permit an uninterrupted appreciation of the architectural elements. The geometric compositions drawn by the intersection of lines and planes are defined by extensive wood moldings and decks. This bright, open interior is an efficient manipulation of a forty-foot-square plan into interesting and adaptable spaces.

A later addition on the back of the house has recently been reworked so that it is more in keeping with the original designs and proportions. The roof pitch, cantilever, and art glass windows now echo the original elements.

Below: The Barr house illustrates how Prairie Style elements were used by other architects. The low sheltering roof with broad overhangs, light screens alternating with solid screens, a horizontal emphasis, and a geometric simplicity are features recognizable in many midwestern communities. Here, the board-and-batten walls draw the home closer to the site, underscoring with their horizontal lines the unity of the elements. [Photographs © Steve Grubman]

Opposite top: The living room's light, neutral color scheme assures that its geometry has no competition. Classic Breuer chairs and a marble dining table contribute their simple shapes.

Opposite bottom: A kitchen renovation maintained the original space but organized it differently, keeping the scale, the flow, and the linear quality. New cabinets match the house's woodwork; familiar wood moldings unite openings.

PURCELL-CUTTS HOUSE

William Gray Purcell grew up not far from Wright's studio in Oak Park but never actually worked there. He did, however, work for Wright's teacher, Louis Sullivan, for a few months in 1903; there, he met George Grant Elmslie, who served as chief draftsman for nearly twenty years. After forming a partnership in Minneapolis in 1907, Purcell and Elmslie became the most prolific of the Prairie School architects, continuing to design in the style after World War I.

Composed for Purcell's own family in 1913, this house in Minneapolis was one of their finest. In 1985 the Anson Cutts family, which had owned it for sixty-six years, bequeathed it to the Minneapolis Institute of Arts, which has undertaken a thorough restoration and opened it to the public.

Elmslie brought a hand well schooled in interior ornamentation to the partnership. The fluid, nature-inspired art glass, stencils, murals, furniture, and carpet designs in their projects were largely his work. Purcell's genius was evident in the layout of their houses. They, too, sought an American architecture that responded to the openness and flexibility of its lifestyle and natural beauty. While it is hard to calculate Wright's influence on their work, Sullivan's inspiration is an undeniable common thread linking them.

A variety of spaces in the long, narrow stucco house are found on several levels. A vaulted ceiling spans the ground-level living room and the second-level dining room before it gives way to the projecting terrace ceiling. Beneath are finely detailed and sometimes whimsical components that all neatly interrelate. A tiny writing nook in a corner of the living room provides a personal space with its own desk. But the fireplace wall was given the greatest attention. The naturalist and the craftsman worked together in wood and brick, paint and glass to accentuate the quiet power of the horizontal line. A triangle motif is repeated in all of the art glass and in some of the furniture. Stencil designs ring the ceiling, some resurrecting the triangle theme. Even the globes of the lights are sponge-painted to blend with the mottled rosy sand walls.

The varied, integral ornament and the extraordinary craftsmanship enhance the function and warmth of the home. The feeling is mellow and unified but more delicate than Wright's interiors.

Opposite, top left: The delicate art glass windows that open up the entire house came from the hand of George Elmslie. These corner examples use the geometric motifs so common in Wright's own designs. As double triangles, the diamonds continue the triangular theme that unites the entire house.

Opposite, top right: Seen from the stencil-lined upstairs hall, the bedroom at left has a compact children's bed, built in like much of Wright's furniture. Oriental rugs add a touch of red to the soft natural tones of both bedrooms, highlighted by the wood paneling and floors. [Photographs by C. M. Korab, Balthazar Korab Ltd.]

Opposite, bottom left and right: Wright's collaborator Richard Bock contributed the sculpture, Nils and His Goose, that perches on the angular storage cabinet between the living and dining rooms. At the writing nook tucked into a corner are a triangular-back chair and a perfectly framed view of a wildflower garden.

Following pages: Charles Livingston Bull's mural of blue herons rises over the fireplace like the moon within its design. The soft mauves, gray, and rose tones set the color palette for the space. Iridescent Tiffany glass glistens in the horizontal joints of the masonry. The oak trim even has a lavender filler beneath its waxed finish.

ERSKINE HOUSE

John S. Van Bergen, an Oak Park native, was one of the last to join Wright's Oak Park studio. He arrived in early 1909 after apprenticing for two years with Walter Burley Griffin, another Wright protégé. Van Bergen also was the last to leave, staying on until 1911 with Isabel Roberts to complete the work that Wright had abandoned when he went to Europe in 1909. After opening his own office in Oak Park, Van Bergen continued to design Prairie Style houses until they went out of fashion during World War I. He is credited with eighteen houses in Oak Park alone between 1912 and 1926, most of them Prairie. Van Bergen was so extremely faithful to the language Wright devised that little of his own creativity is apparent in many of his works. After the war, a return to more traditional styles left most designers who had been seeking a new American architecture scrambling for work. Van Bergen moved to Chicago's north shore, where he designed many interesting houses, and eventually went to California, where he practiced until he was eighty years old.

Van Bergen drew heavily on Wright's design for a "Fireproof House for $5,000," which was published in the *Ladies' Home Journal* in 1906. Later, he borrowed ideas from the American System Built Homes that Wright designed for the Richards Company in Milwaukee. The 1913 house in Oak Park built for lawyer Robert Erskine and his family was typical of Van Bergen's versions of the "Fireproof House." Intended to be poured concrete, it was stucco on wood frame instead. Its compact, thirty-foot-square plan fits neatly on the urban grid for which it was designed. Beneath a low hipped roof are a living room, dining room, and kitchen on the first floor and three bedrooms and a bathroom on the second. An early addition included a first-floor den and bathroom and an extra bedroom to the rear.

No space is wasted. It is efficient and economical yet offers many of the distinctive features of larger Prairie Style houses. A sheltering porch provides a welcome at the side entrance, easing the transition inside. Van Bergen varied the plan by placing the entrance between the living and dining areas rather than between the kitchen and living room. A large, rectilinear fireplace marks the center of the house, with bands of art glass windows defining the perimeters. The wood stripping on the exterior and interior walls emphasizes the rectangular forms that are repeated throughout. Leading the eye horizontally from one space to another, they attempt to destroy the box as much as possible, giving the illusion of much grander spaces.

Opposite top: The current owners have found a suitable setting for their extensive collection of Arts and Crafts furniture and ceramics. Selected pieces of Mission oak furniture, including Stickley items, have been purchased at auctions and from antiques dealers. Newly designed dining room furniture, inspired by the Robie house chairs, was integrated into the room.

Opposite bottom: Arts and Crafts pottery, so popular when the home was built, fills the shelves with geometric shapes and colorful glazes. Most were made by Marblehead, but Teco, Grueby, and Rookwood also are represented. The cool greens and blues are a perfect accent to the golden Prairie interior. [Photographs by Chester Brummel]

SCHINDLER HOUSE

One of the few apprentices who worked with Wright during the transition between the Oak Park studio and the Taliesin Fellowship was Viennese architect Rudolph M. Schindler. Schindler and his wife, Pauline, were inspired by Taliesin's unified experience of work and play in a natural setting. In 1920 Schindler went to Los Angeles to supervise the Barnsdall projects for Wright, but by 1921 he had established his own practice. Its base until his death in 1953 was this innovative home and studio in West Hollywood.

Designed and built that first year jointly by the Schindlers and their close friends, Clyde and Marian Chase, the complex incorporates some distinct Wright influences as well as new poured-concrete technologies with which Chase was familiar. Like Wright's buildings, it is based on a unit system organized into flexible, inspiring spaces and is intimately related to its site. While the use of walls of doors that open to outside gardens is similar to Wright's treatment of the Hollyhock house, many of the Schindler house's techniques predate applications by Wright in his later Usonian designs.

The most radical departure from traditional plans was the owners' scheme for cooperative living. As Schindler described it:

The basic idea was to give each person his own room—instead of the usual distribution—and to do most of the cooking right at the table—making it more a social "campfire" affair, than the disagreeable burden to one member of the family. . . . Each room represents a variation on one structural and architectural theme. . . . the basic requirement for a camper's shelter: a protected back, an open front, a fireplace and a roof.

Open-air sleeping was accommodated by a rooftop porch, and a guest wing was included to provide rental income.

The house is built of durable and easy-to-maintain concrete and has a gravel roof. Employing what Schindler called his slab-tilt system, the forms were constructed horizontally; then the concrete was poured, finished, and left to dry, following which the slabs were tilted into vertical positions with a block and tackle. The spaces left when the forms were removed were filled with concrete or glass.

The couples built their own furniture over several years, then the Chases left in 1924 and were replaced by the family of Richard Neutra, another Viennese architect who also had worked briefly with Wright. For a long time, this communal home typified the creative, progressive ideologies discussed within its walls.

Opposite top: Movable partitions and patio walls are simple screens of wood with glass or Insulite.

Opposite bottom: Patios and sunken gardens create extended and defined outdoor living areas adjoining each room, with outdoor fireplaces reinforcing the concept of an actual living room.

Above: Bamboo hedges protect the privacy of the 100-by-200-foot site, which since 1980 has been owned by the Friends of the Schindler House. The cool gray of the concrete is complemented by redwood tones used in posts and ceilings. Copper fireplace hoods pick up the color inside. [Photographs © Grant Mudford]

DOW STUDIO

Early in life, Alden Dow, son of the founder of the Dow Chemical Company, demonstrated a fondness for and a sensitivity to design. In fact, he was drawn to architecture when he stayed at Wright's Imperial Hotel as a child, visiting Japan with his parents. Like Wright, he dabbled in photography as a means of recording the images of life in a composed format. Soon after graduation from Columbia University's school of architecture, he and his wife, Vada, spent a memorable five months at Taliesin in 1933. There, Dow found someone who shared his interest in nature, in the relationship of a building's materials to its design, and in the impact of a building on its occupants—a kindred spirit.

He soon opened his own studio in Midland, Michigan, where he practiced architecture until his death in 1983. Dow named his design philosophy "composed order." It recognized, he explained, "that there may be many good answers put together in a variety of ways and that truly great results come from an organic or growable idea on which smaller contributions can develop. The ideal is to achieve harmony among the people, materials and ideas involved." He was so admired for his contribution to his home state that he was named its architect laureate in 1983. The Alden B. Dow Creativity Center was founded to perpetuate his commitment to quality and innovation.

Like Wright, Dow focused his career on residential architecture. Over the years he designed sixty homes in Midland and many others elsewhere in the country. During the 1930s he built thirteen houses using a patented system called Unit Blocks. Among them was his own home and studio in Midland, built between 1937 and 1940.

There is no better example of his philosophy or his ability to intermingle nature and architecture than this inspiring composition.

The one-foot-square Unit Blocks were cast from recycled cinders from the Dow Chemical Company. He used them not only to form walls and terraces beneath the broad copper roof; they also took their place ornamentally in the surrounding pond, like stepping stones. Water is often an integral part of Dow's designs. Here, the pond he created stops just short of his studio, separated only by two layers of blocks. A conference room in the reception area, often called the submarine room, is actually two feet below the pond's surface. When the suns reflects off the water into the room, it dances on the walls. The porch and other rooms overlook the pond. Interior spaces flow quietly into the garden. There is hardly a pause where one meets the other.

Custom built-in furniture and other decorative arts that were designed or selected for the rooms maintain the geometry and the rhythm of the building. Modular stools can be pulled out from beneath multilevel tables to provide extra seating. Woven plastic strips conceal lighting in the living room ceiling. Unlike Wright, Dow used generous amounts of bright colors. Vibrant, clear hues contrast with white-painted cinder blocks throughout the complex, creating an excitement that challenges the serenity of the gracious spaces. The bright green carpet in one living room area yields to red in the next. Multicolored cushions dot the sofa. In Dow's office, multiple planes overlap in the ceiling, each another pure color—red, green, hot pink, purple, yellow. As Dow urged, "Separate parts put together so each part contributes the most to the others."

Opposite: Overlooking the pond, the living room of Alden Dow's studio is a rainbow of color. Painted cinder blocks provide a multidimensional backdrop for the splashes of gold, red, pink, and green. Dow was much more aggressive and experimental with his use of color than Wright. [Photographs by Balthazar Korab]

Dow shared Wright's love of red and appreciation for the simplicity of Japanese design, a fact that is evident in interior details as well as in the landscaping. This bridge shows his masterful ability to integrate fabricated elements with the natural. His use of a red linear design against the greenery is reminiscent of the gates at Taliesin.

The home and studio gradually takes form beyond the pond, its Unit Blocks gathered together beneath a low, angular roof. The integration of building and site is complete. Sixty-seven acres of magnificently landscaped gardens surround Dow's home and have evolved over nearly a century. Guests are welcome to amble through the botanical park, which offers with the change of each season new insights into the cooperation between nature and architecture.

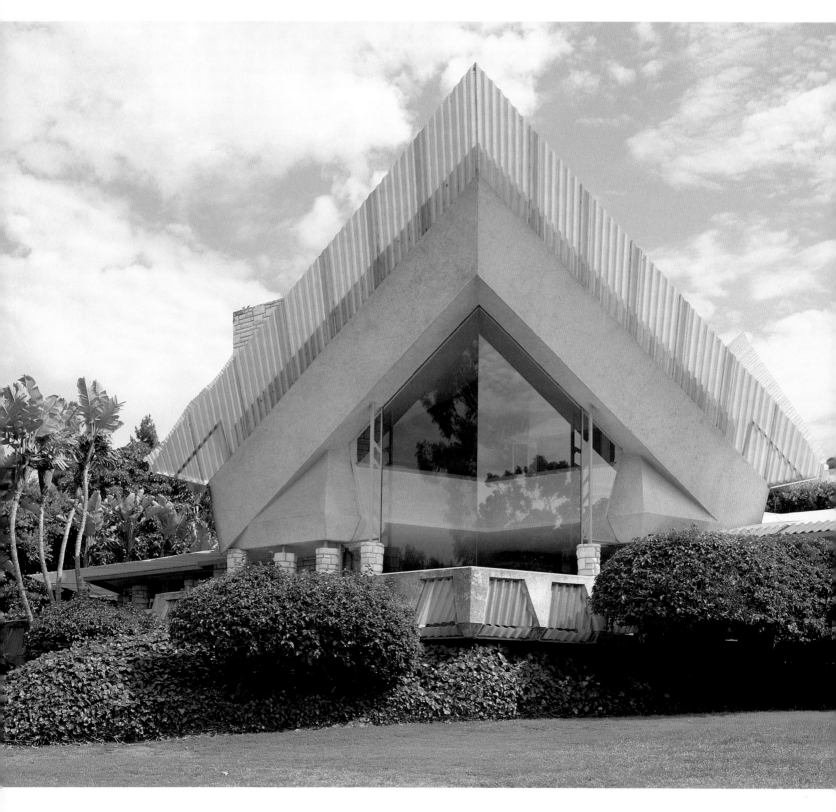

BOWLER HOUSE

Lloyd Wright, actually Frank Lloyd Wright, Jr., the oldest child of the Oak Park family, was born the year in which Catherine and Frank moved into their home, 1889. As a young man he traveled to Italy to help his father prepare the drawings for the famous German publication of Wright's work produced by Ernst Wasmuth in 1910–1911. He was trained as a landscape architect in the office of the noted landscape architects Olmsted and Olmsted and later worked for Irving Gill, a California architect who did pioneering work in concrete technology.

From 1920 to 1925, while his father was traveling back and forth to Japan and later to the Midwest, Lloyd Wright supervised most of the California concrete block commissions then under construction, a project that proved frustrating given the elder Wright's inaccessibility. However, Lloyd Wright continued to experiment with concrete construction throughout the 1920s. His designs were often richly ornamented and imaginative, well suited to his California clientele. He practiced architecture and landscape design in the Los Angeles area until his death in 1978. His most well-known commission was the Wayfarers Chapel of 1951 in Palos Verdes.

John Bowler, a contractor for industrial buildings, had heard of Lloyd Wright through another client. Bowler needed a large family home for his four growing boys in Palos Verdes. In 1963 Lloyd Wright produced a fanciful form, somewhat like an exotic bird that has just landed on a rock ledge. Its reinforced concrete deck and slab, together with the wood-frame and stucco walls, establish a solid base for the complex plan, which is based on a diamond module. An unusual roof system of built-up roofing on a wood frame, with a thin layer of pumice concrete on top to protect it, has proven to be durable while maintaining the uniform texture of the walls.

Lloyd Wright, of course, beautifully landscaped the entire site and designed all of the furniture for the living and dining rooms. Velveteen upholstery on the seating pieces repeats the yellow-green tones of a geometric-patterned screen in the living room. Angles continue throughout the home. Mirrors in the bathroom are faceted like a crystal. The fireplace and rhythmic columns are a tan Arizona sandstone. The travertine floor was a later, but compatible, addition.

In the Bowler house, the architect was given the opportunity and freedom to create a total unity, inside and out, providing a durable and inspiring home base for the venturesome family.

Opposite: The tan color and aggregate texture of the Bowler house confirm its close relationship to the earth. Grooved industrial plastic "plummage," however, soars beyond the roof, its blue color blending with the California sky. The decorated geometric parapet rail on the first-floor deck is reinforced concrete.

Above: An elaborate screen in the living room, partially attached to the wall, is loosely based on an abstraction of a bird of paradise. Diamond and triangular shapes were formed by walnut strips filled in with anodized aluminum and plastic in gold, mossy green, and white. [Photographs by Alan Weintraub]

HOWE HOUSE

For twenty-seven years John Howe worked at the side of Frank Lloyd Wright, directing the activities of his drafting room and completing many of Wright's presentation drawings. As one of the first members of the Taliesin Fellowship, he was well schooled in the principles of organic architecture. After Wright's death, he established a successful practice in Minneapolis, where, like Wright, he has focused on houses.

John and Lu Howe's own 1971 home, Sankaku, the Japanese term for an equilateral triangle, is nestled in a hillside overlooking a small wooded lake in Burnsville. The triangle gives the home not just its name but also its energy and repose. The approach to the concealed front door is down a naturally landscaped path, onto a deck, across a bridge. Inside, a narrow hallway leads at an angle to open, multilevel spaces that embrace their natural setting. Down a few stairs, the living, dining, and kitchen areas open to the lake view. Porches enhance the rooms spatially and aesthetically, drawing one's vision and activities beyond the walls. The two bedrooms are on the entry level, and a sanctum—like a treehouse—rests among the branches at the top. Half walls are used when full-height walls are not needed, opening the spaces one to another.

While compact, the house feels spacious because it borrows space, visually, from outside and is not compartmentalized. Soft light reflecting from light decks adds to the serenity of the living room. The triangle reappears like an old friend in light fixtures, art glass, furniture, stairway treads, and porches. It is reformulated into hexagons for tables and cutout designs in the light deck.

All of the furniture was designed by Howe, but it bears a close resemblance to familiar Wright designs. The long bench, triangular lounge chairs, and straight dining chairs all are scaled perfectly to suit their purpose and their space. The gold and tangerine upholstery is a nubby, basket weave in contrast to the hard, clean lines and smooth Philippine mahogany surfaces. Carefully selected accessories project a love for fine craftsmanship and a respect for the artisan. Simple Japanese art draws attention to a wall or a shelf. The efficiency of the spaces is so enhanced by the personal interests of the owners that the house radiates an inherent glow of harmony.

Like so many of Wright's own houses, here the fireplace is at the core, reaching for the roof. The distinctively Wrightian table lamps are modeled on a Taliesin design. [Les Turnau]

GERINGER HOUSE

Arthur Dyson apprenticed with architects Bruce Goff and William Gray Purcell as well as Frank Lloyd Wright. From them he extracted a personal style that enables him to create original spaces from the unique needs and characters of his clients. Like Wright, the dry inventory of clients' needs is not as important as knowing what gives them pleasure, what aspects of nature they admire, and what the attributes of their site are. "Architecture is a philosophy towards life," he says, "an avenue which originates with living individuals and their requirements—incorporating everything from the pragmatism of resisting the elements to the poetry of ideals and dreams, and undertakes to provide a setting to awaken senses, to stimulate imagination and to expand consciousness in a world in harmony with its environment."

When asked to design a house in Kerman, California, for Ralph and Nancy Geringer, Dyson, now based in Fresno, found that this young farming couple with two sons wanted a home that would separate them from the fields of grapes that dominated their days. They desired a private shelter, horizontal and rustic in feeling, that would give them visual access to the views but protect them from the sun and wind and farm activities.

What they got, in 1979, was a farmhouse-in-the-round. The circular home, raised above the land, makes room for a lush oasis in its center court. A swimming pool, spa, and generous plantings on surrounding terraces contrast with the dusty fields outside their walls. All division walls radiate from the center.

The kitchen opens to the game room and overlooks the pool. An overhead trellis holds pots and pans and repeats the trellises that are used elsewhere to filter light and link areas. Generous windows open the home to the center, offering terraces for indoor-outdoor living. Interior spaces are varied, some with high, soaring ceilings, others with low, intimate ones. Hidden corners throughout the house offer special views. Light streams through clerestory windows but allows privacy. The trellises and low roofs intensify movement in some areas, while others, such as the living rooms, emerge as open pools of space. The board-and-batten walls and cedar-shingled roof create interesting compositions as they curve and turn and shelter from the sun.

Opposite: An aerial view of the Geringer residence reveals the uniqueness of the site. Carved out of the flat surrounding fields, it is a private refuge, an innovative response to a farming family's needs.

Above: The round plan includes an interior garden court, pool, and spa. All rooms open to this pleasant oasis. The gentle curves and open but varied spaces within the home break the monotony of the row-after-row panorama of the family's daily work. [Photographs by Scot Zimmerman]

EDMONDSON HOUSE

The short time E. Fay Jones spent at Taliesin in 1953 left an indelible imprint on his life's work. As an apprentice who was a graduate of Rice University's architecture school, he quickly absorbed Wright's principles of organic architecture; they have guided his work into breathtaking directions. He has inspired emerging architects at the University of Arkansas for nearly forty years. His understanding of nature's systems and materials, his ability to translate them into forms responding to a client's needs, and his meticulous attention to detail have produced an abundance of award-winning buildings and the Gold Medal of the American Institute of Architects for himself.

The house Jones designed in 1979 for Don and Ellen Edmondson in Forest City, Arkansas, not far from the architect's office in Fayetteville, came about from careful analysis of the clients' desires and the potential of the dramatic site. The mutual trust among clients, architect, and an able builder produced a magnificent house that rises four levels within the trees on Crowley's Ridge, high above a lake.

Gracefully rooted to its site, the house is layered into the hillside like the dogwood that surrounds it. Broad horizontal tile roofs anchor the building, while creamy stucco walls and rich redwood details reach for the treetops. The clients preferred a more tailored look than stone would have given. They chose stucco, which offers a canvas for patterns cast by branches and leaves—using the trees to provide natural ornamentation.

Jones, with his associate on the house, Maurice Jennings, designed the outdoor sculptures, furniture, lamps, pottery, table linens, and even stationery so that the experience of living in the home would be harmonious. An E-shaped motif emerged from the structural elements and became an abstract pattern that reappears in various places such as the clerestory windows and the intricate trellis that connects the house to the guest house, a recent addition.

The living room is actually a series of indoor and outdoor spaces including a screened porch and a large deck. Ceiling levels reach up two stories, then drop down over more intimate areas. Accents of color—red, orange, blue—dot all of the rooms in pillows and cushions, like wildflowers in a meadow. Mirrors echo the natural light and subtle details, multiplying their effect. In the same way, the house serves as a mirror, echoing the fundamental geometry and simplicity of nature.

Opposite: On the fourth level of the house is the study, overlooking the bedroom above the living area. The neutral palette of the furnishings and the walls spotlights the detail and fine craftsmanship of the wood trim, which is redwood, while the cabinetry is a clear-finished red oak.

Above: The house is entered, gradually, at the second level, by passing through a gate, then through a courtyard and over a bridge. The varied planes, the seductive spaces, and nature's arms seem to point the way. The challenges of the steep site were well rewarded. [Photographs by R. Greg Hursley]

SEGEL HOUSE

Since studying with Wright for six years at Taliesin, John Lautner has earned international acclaim for his individualized architectural solutions. According to Lautner, the purpose of architecture is to improve human life, not to promote a particular style. He points to Gottfried Semper's "Four Elements of Architecture": the moral and spiritual element; the roof; the enclosure; the mound or foundation. From them Lautner creates sculptural forms for living. Based in Los Angeles for the past fifty years, his designs—often exciting engineering feats as well as artistic compositions—are concentrated on the West Coast.

Gil and Joanne Segel, a dance therapist, wanted something soaring, yet of the ground. It was to be solid and free, built of wood. Joanne Segel's collaboration with the architect yielded an undulating beach cave of wood, glass, and stone. The cooperation between client and architect is apparent in the unity of this design in Malibu, California, completed in 1979.

The orientation is up and down the beach, not a flat, panoramic view out to sea like many of its neighbors. The sweep of the sandy beach on one side, seen through an uninterrupted curved wall of glass, and the private garden on the other lift the spirit while rooting it to the earth. The three-inch edges of Douglas fir timbers that form the partially hyperbolic-shaped roof create a rhythm in the ceiling of the living room that appears to radiate from the round, poured-concrete fireplace at the corner. Boulders rising from the rock floor are mimicked by the soft irregular forms of the sofas the owner had fabricated. Natural cottons and linens in light creams and beiges provide the neutrality desired—because nature provides so many colors through the windows. The motor court adjoining the living room is designed so that when the cars are removed, it becomes a stone-floored entertainment area.

Upstairs, the dance studio is a celebration of curves accentuated by light patterns from trellised ceiling panels. Walls of concrete, which was used for soundproofing, have been covered with wood.

Every room has a view of the ocean. To improve the bedroom view, the roof of the living room was covered with green grass, concealing the roofing material. It is no wonder that Lautner refers to his practice as "mostly private homes hidden from sight."

Opposite top: The hyperbolic curve of the roof matches the rolling curves of the hills and rocks of Malibu's beach. Inside and out, the home is an extension of the landscape that is visible from its rooms. [Julius Shulman]

Below: The lush marble shower area combines natural tones of red on the outside and brown within. Wood paneling and rock forms that surround it create the quiet feeling of a private waterfall in a secluded forest. [Alan Weintraub]

Following pages: The contours of the house and the boulders outside it are repeated in the living room space and the shapes within it. Views looking toward the ocean to the left or the private garden to the right are framed by the walls and become decorative elements. [Julius Shulman]

Opposite, bottom left and right: Curves continue the motif of the house, from a black pool off the deck to a bar area surrounding a fireplace. The ocean's reflection in the glass further underscores the house's relationship to its site. [Alan Weintraub]

BENTON HOUSE

A community of architects who apprenticed with Wright until his death in 1959 continues to practice organic architecture, under the name Taliesin Architects, Ltd., from bases in Wisconsin and Arizona. Organized as a subsidiary of the Frank Lloyd Wright Foundation, they carry on the tradition of teaching while working. Over the past thirty years Taliesin Architects has completed hundreds of projects scattered throughout the world. William Wesley Peters, the first Taliesin apprentice, served as the senior architect until his death in 1991. He also was the designer for the finely composed Benton house in Malibu, California, begun in 1981.

John Benton was a long-time friend of the Wright family when he commissioned a new home for his wife, Melinda, and family that also had to accommodate their extensive collection of American art. Their five-acre, sloping site ends abruptly at a bluff overlooking the Pacific Ocean, projecting out beyond the adjoining land.

The architect's response was an L-shaped plan that placed all living spaces—the living–dining room, the study, and four bedrooms—parallel to the cliff edge, offering free views of the beach and the ocean to the south. Perpendicular to this sixty-foot wing is the service area, which includes a garage, entry, kitchen, maid's room, and office. Long, broad stairs drop slowly toward the cliff edge on one side. A curved terrace projects over the ledge on the other side.

Although based on a sixteen-inch grid (used alternately with a four-foot variation), the design is marked by a forceful triangular motif that is articulated in the pitch and jagged edges of the roof, garden shapes, lights, window and door mullions, and projections at either end of the plan. A third shape, a circle, creates garden motifs, a pool at the entrance, a terrace wall, and the roof tiles. The interplay of geometric shapes is skillfully composed.

Top: In the dining and other areas, floor-to-ceiling glass walls open the home to generous terraces and a lush landscape. Caramel leather furniture and natural red oak tones in tables and cabinets harmonize with the warm color of the plaster. Scores of native American baskets rest on the horizontal decks that span the rooms.

Right: The clients' immense library was taken into consideration when the architets developed the plan for the house. Colorful ribbons of books lining the walls became striking decorative elements. There to be enjoyed, the books are easily found and read in the well-lit area. [Photographs by Taliesin Architects, Ltd.]

Above: Red squares in the court-yard are a reminder of the house's module. Vertigris copper coating on the window frames echoes the deep green color of the ocean. Combined with the cobalt blue roof, the palette of the exterior is decidedly more polychromatic than the subtle interior.

Following pages: The blue of the tile roof, the house's dominant design element, exaggerates the bright blue of the California sky and rolls like the ocean. The muted peach plaster that covers the concrete-block and wood walls is drawn from the tone of the land and is a complementary back-ground inside for Navajo rugs and carefully placed drawings and prints. Construction of the house was a five-year project directed by John Benton. The meticulous exe-cution of every detail, including custom-fabricated frames sur-rounding 641 window panes, yards of cabinetry, installation of 276 built-in light fixtures, ceiling marking strips, and light decks, was all coordinated and supervised by the owner himself.

FIJHER HOUJE

Originally from Wright's native Wisconsin, Milton Stricker joined the Taliesin Fellowship in 1952 after studying architecture at Carnegie-Mellon University. From Wright he learned the language of organic architecture, which he has practiced from Seattle for nearly forty years. The simplicity of his forms has allowed him to produce exquisite residences that respond to the site and the client's distinctive requirements yet are economical.

One of Stricker's larger commissions is the 1989 retirement home for Jean and Frank Fisher. They selected a site in a newly subdivided area that had been a ranch in Sisters, Oregon. Wagon trains once passed by on the nearby Oregon Trail. The area's history and Jean Fisher's native American ancestry led the architect to create a design symbolically reflecting this combined heritage. He proposed a tepee-shaped living area in a plan based on a hexagonal module.

The 3,200 square feet of space is enveloped in beveled cedar siding that alternates wide and narrow bands. The broad cedar-shake roof is an earthy companion to the rock-strewn terrain, marked by tall ponderosa pines and sagebrush. An old pine snag, or stump, on the site became the source of the house's color scheme; within its weathered rings were shades of tan and gold, orange, and even red. A local salishan stone was massed for the towering central fireplace and supporting piers.

An angled garage wing joins the house to create the entrance. Inside, the open plan reveals itself. No corridors waste space. The living room reaches to the top of the tepee shape, anchored by the fireplace. Built-in and free-standing furniture designed for the home continues the flow. It is a complete design, one Wright would no doubt have recognized as grown from the seeds he planted so long ago.

Opposite: Looking from the den into the open living area, the fluidity and unity of the spaces are clear. Triangular shapes produced by the house's hexagonal module create unusual interconnected and dynamic rooms. The living area soars to the top of its tepee ceiling and out like a ship's prow.

Top: Horizontal courses of beveled cedar siding emphasize the outreaching angular forms.

Bottom: A triangular master bathroom opens through french doors to the terrace and ponderosa pines beyond. [Photographs by Randy Shelton, Architectural Images]

Radiating from the center of a salishan stone fireplace is a decorative ceiling light screen—an abstraction of the nearby Sisters mountain range, the town of Sisters, and the profile of the residence itself.

The massive fireplace rises to the top of the living room ceiling, clearly defining the hearth as the center of the house. Modular hassocks and benches, upholstered in golds and pumpkins, are clustered in various places on the wool Berber carpet. Cove lighting produces an indirect glow from the cedar-covered ceiling, while companion fixtures point down to light various areas directly.

WRIGHT AT HOME

THIS CATALOGUE PRESENTS AN ARRAY OF UNIQUE HOME FURNISHINGS THAT MAY BE PURCHASED TODAY: REPRODUCTIONS OF ORIGINAL WRIGHT DESIGNS, INSPIRATIONS FROM THEM, AND ITEMS THAT ARE COMPATIBLE WITH THE WRIGHT STYLE. DECORATIVE ARTS SUPPLIERS ARE LISTED ON PAGE 217.

Trellised Vine Fabric
Glencoe Window Fabric
Wisteria Foliage Velvet Fabric
Various materials and colorways
Nos. 25335, 43230, 43222
Schumacher

After the editor of *House Beautiful* urged Wright to bring his design ideas within reach of average consumers, Wright in 1955 launched his Taliesin Line in the magazine's pages. Schumacher was among the first companies to translate his concepts into commercial products, including fabrics and wallpapers. More than a half century later, it continues to offer a changing Wright collection. New patterns have been inspired by the architect's famed art glass designs, his passion for nature, and his own personal collection of Japanese prints and other works of art.

Imperial Tokyo Armchair
(above left)
Imperial Hotel, 1916–22
Cherry base in natural, walnut,
or black
Fabric or leather upholstery
29½" high, 37½" wide, 36⅛" deep
No. 622
Cassina USA

Imperial Tokyo Sofa *(above right)*
Imperial Hotel, 1916–22
Cherry base in natural, walnut,
or black
Fabric or leather upholstery
29½" high, 81½" wide, 36⅛" deep
(three seats, shown)
29½" high, 59½" wide, 36⅛" deep
(two seats)
No. 622
Cassina USA

One of Wright's most important commissions, the Imperial Hotel in Tokyo has now vanished except for ruins of the lobby reconstructed at an outdoor museum—and some of his most inventive furnishings. This padded sofa and armchair convey a streamlined moderne look that contrasts with Wright's more rectilinear Prairie Style furnishings from the previous decade. Other distinctive furniture designed for the Imperial Hotel include a series of armless oak side chairs whose hexagonal backs mimicked the peaked rise of the ceiling in the "peacock alley" promenade.

Prairie Settle with Table Arms
(below)
Robie House, 1908
Various woods, finishes, and
upholstery
27" high, 93" wide, 45¾" deep
No. 2252
Swartzendruber Hardwood
Creations

With its strong horizontal lines that seem to hug the earth, Wright's house for the Frederick C. Robie family is one of his finest Prairie designs. Inside are free-flowing spaces: the living room and dining room, giving the impression of

being a single open space, are separated only by a two-sided fireplace. The furnishings were designed in cooperation with George Mann Niedecken to enhance the same feeling of openness. Adapted from a piece created for the Robie house, this two-seat sofa with extended arm rests, a behind-the-seat shelf, and an upholstered seat reflects the dominant horizontals of the residence itself (pages 46–47). Its unique design eliminates the need for accompanying end or back tables. The slightly flared leg is consistent with other details in the house. Either paneled or slatted wood sides are available.

Barrel Chair
Darwin Martin House, 1904
Cherry in natural or walnut
Various fabrics
32" high, 21½" wide, 22" deep
No. 606
Cassina USA

Wright designed the first version of this chair, made of oak, for the Darwin Martins' house (page 79) about 1904. This later version was produced for Herbert Johnson's home, Wingspread, in Racine, Wisconsin, in 1937 (page 102). When Wright saw the chairs, he ordered a dozen for his own living room at Taliesin (pages 60–61). There they form a scalloped edge around his ruggedly rectangular dining table, their slats matching the ends of the table.

Prairie Easy Chair
Various woods, finishes, and upholstery
27" high, 40¾" wide, 38" deep
No. 2250
Swartzendruber Hardwood Creations

A companion to the Prairie Settle with Table Arms, this comfortable armchair recalls a number of sturdy pieces designed for Wright's early houses. The all-enveloping boxy lines were a perfect match for his Prairie Style commissions.

Hillside Theater Curtain Pillow
Taliesin, 1953 *(below left)*
Cotton tapestry, polyester fill
17" square
No. PL/67291
WrightStyle

Like Wright's stylized art glass, a new curtain he designed for the Hillside Theater at Taliesin tells a story of nature in his own geometric language, describing the land around his home: its brown fields, red barns, green hills, and the blackbirds that fly overhead. This pillow reproduces the vibrant tones and shapes of the original. Other pillows based on Wright designs are also available.

Coonley 1 Chair
Coonley House, 1907
Cherry in natural, walnut, or black
Various fabrics
27½" high, 17" wide, 18½" deep
No. 609
Cassina USA

Designed for the Avery Coonleys' house, one of Wright's most complex and beautifully articulated residences, this chair is similar to those Wright designed for the Dana, Husser, and Clark houses as well as for his own use. This version, with an upholstered seat and slatted back, is shorter and has a less formal appearance than the 37-inch-high Coonley 2 Chair (page 196).

Lake Geneva Magazine Rack *(right)*
Lake Geneva Inn, 1911
Cast aluminum in dark bronze finish
13" high, 11" wide, 12" deep
No. MR/420551
WrightStyle

A window in this small Wisconsin resort hotel, since demolished, inspired this metal magazine rack. Diamonds and other geometric shapes join together to form an abstraction resembling a tulip, a floral motif Wright had used previously for windows in his own home.

Purcell Chair
Purcell-Cutts House, 1913
Quartersawn white oak
Leather upholstery
33⅛" high, 24⅛" wide, 22" deep
Peter Korab Studios

Two chairs designed by Purcell and Elmslie for this house (pages 160–61) were reproduced when it was restored by the Minneapolis Institute of Arts. Both have thirty-four spindles and dozens of little blocks, but the half-back version has only a small upholstered pad on the back. Duplicates are available to benefit further restoration efforts.

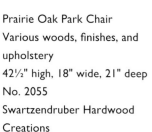

Prairie Oak Park Chair
Various woods, finishes, and upholstery
42½" high, 18" wide, 21" deep
No. 2055
Swartzendruber Hardwood Creations

One of the first pieces of furniture that Wright designed was a simple wooden chair with a back that slides down past the seat to rest on the bottom stretcher. This reinterpretation of Wright's "machine to sit in," as the architect later described his early chairs, substitutes slats for the solid board that he used originally. The adaptation has a wide crest rail, detail around the seat rails, and flared feet.

Robie 1 Chair
Robie House, 1908
Cherry in natural, walnut, or black
Fabric or leather upholstery
52½" high, 16" wide, 18" deep
No. 601
Cassina USA

Wright liked to use slatted screens throughout his houses to mark a separation without closing off space. This dramatic high-back side or dining chair with vertical wood slats offered a contrast to the strongly horizontal lines of the Robie house. When all the chairs were grouped at the table, they created a "room within a room."

Dana-Thomas Chair
Dana-Thomas House, 1902
Oak
Leather upholstery
51" high, 17" wide, 18" deep
Dana-Thomas House Foundation

This stately, vertical slat-back dining room chair is a reproduction of originals that Wright designed for Susan Lawrence Dana's elegant house, where she entertained frequently in the dramatic dining space (page 71). Also available from the foundation is a reproduction of a small oak dining table like those Wright designed to extend the house's dining capacity. It has a cantilevered square top with vertical slats on two sides of the base and connecting cross stretchers.

Wright Floor Clock
Booth House, 1915
Alder in a natural finish
66" high, 10" wide, 16½" deep
No. C3326
Bulova

Based on a print stand Wright designed for a 1908 exhibition of his work, this piece was later adapted for the Glencoe, Illinois, home of his attorney, Sherman Booth—one of only three free-standing light fixtures Wright ever designed. A clock face has replaced the light; below that, a shelf and a stepped base frame a row of slats to match Wright's famous chairs.

Reader's Table *(above)*
Oil-finished cherry
30" high, 110" or 134" long,
48" wide
Thos. Moser Cabinetmakers

Inspired by Wright's furniture, this generous dining room or library table features a series of three parallel posts that create a Prairie look. It is well suited to a large space and can be paired with the company's Reader's Side Chair, which was designed to complement the table. The chair has a medium-high slatted back and an upholstered seat, which is available in leather or a choice of fabric.

Allen Table *(below)*
Allen House, 1917
Cherry in natural or walnut
27¾" high, 101¼" or 110¼" long,
41¾" wide
No. 605
Cassina USA

The cantilevered horizontal lines of this table designed for the Henry J. Allens are typical of Wright's Prairie Style furniture. Two versions seat six or eight persons. Shown around the table are the tall slat-back chairs (opposite) designed for the Robie house. "Human beings must group, sit or recline, confound them—and they must dine," Wright wrote in his 1932 *Autobiography,* "but dining is much easier to manage and always was a great artistic opportunity."

Taliesin 2 Dining Table (above)
Taliesin, 1925
Cherry in natural or walnut
27½" high, 75½" or 98" long,
38½" wide
No. 608
Cassina USA

Coonley 2 Chair (above and right)
Coonley House, 1907
Cherry in natural, walnut, or black
Various fabrics
37" high, 17" wide, 18½" deep
No. 614
Cassina USA

Wright designed this table for his own use in the area that served as both living room and dining room at Taliesin in Spring Green, Wisconsin (pages 60–61). The table, shown in walnut, is surrounded by a quartet of medium-high-back Coonley 2 Chairs as well as a pair of Wright's Barrel Chairs (page 193), which were his choice at Taliesin; there they added contrasting shapes against the backdrop of his home's natural limestone walls, producing a dynamic yet cozy alcove nestled in the large open area where the Wrights gathered.

Husser Dining Table (below)
Husser House, 1889
Cherry in natural or walnut
29" high, 60" long, 50" wide
No. 615
Cassina USA

Located in Chicago on the shore of Lake Michigan, Wright's Husser house (razed in 1926) pointed the way to the Prairie Style that occupied the next decade and a half of his career. While looking forward, it also harked back to the work of Wright's mentor, Louis Sullivan, displaying a Sullivanesque exterior frieze that called attention to the sweeping roof above. Similar fretwork appeared on the Hussers' dining table, adding interest to the deep edges. Four massive legs support the square-looking table and sandwich slatted screens on the ends—a prototype for the dining table he would design for Taliesin in 1925. With their slat backs, Coonley 2 Chairs in a matching natural cherry finish complement the handsome table.

Taliesin 2 Dining Table
(above and right)
Taliesin, 1925
Cherry in natural or walnut
27½" high, 75½" or 98" long,
38½" wide
No. 608
Cassina USA

This striking rectangular table was used by the Wright family and their continual flow of guests from 1925 to 1959. Its slatted sides create a screen while letting light through. (At Taliesin the table is covered in glass to catch reflections.) The table is shown here in the natural cherry finish with complementary low-back Coonley 1 Chairs (page 193).

Aurora Sideboard *(below left)*
Greene House, 1912
Cherry in natural or walnut
28½" or 43" high, 86" wide,
22½" deep
No. 624
Cassina USA

Now completely finished on all sides for use as a freestanding unit, the original of this sideboard was built into the dining room of one of Wright's late Prairie houses in Aurora, Illinois. Its simple lines reflect the rhythm of the house's facade itself—fulfilling the architect's belief that furnishings should be "mere structural details" of a building's overall character. "It is quite impossible to consider the building one thing and its furnishings another," he wrote in 1910. This reproduction is available as the base unit only, as shown, or including a cantilevered top piece with five narrow drawers.

May Desk *(above left)*
May House, 1908
Cherry in natural, walnut, or black
29" high, 45¼" wide, 24½" deep
No. 619
Cassina USA

Furnishings for the May house were executed in cooperation with the "interior architect" George Mann Niedecken of Milwaukee, a frequent collaborator on Wright's projects. This exquisite writing desk is equipped with two drawers and a top rack. Developed with the Milwaukee Art Museum.

Robie 2 Tables *(below left)*
Robie House, 1908
Cherry in natural, walnut, or black
16" high, 14" or 35½" square
No. 610
Cassina USA

Part of Wright's furnishings plan for the Robie house included these versatile cocktail or coffee tables, including a small one that doubles as a stool. The larger table is available with a wood or a glass top. Each design reflects the dramatic cantilevers of the house itself, with flared legs to match the sofa with table arms in the Robie house.

Lewis Coffee Tables *(below right)*
Lewis House, 1939
Cherry in natural, walnut, or black
16" high, 35" or 45" square
No. 623
Cassina USA

The architect refined his double-shelf table concept into his Usonian years, developing this strikingly cantilevered example for the house of his friend Lloyd Lewis in Liberty-ville, Illinois. Traditional legs have been forsaken for perpendicular slats that anchor the bottom and hold the top shelf aloft—mimicking Wright's flat roofs and miniaturiz-ing the Lewis house itself.

Taliesin Pagoda-Shade Lamps
(above right)
Taliesin, 1925
Cherry in natural, wine, walnut, or black with laminated paper shade
20" high, 14" wide, 16" deep
11¼" high, 12¾" wide, 16" deep
Nos. 2306, 2526
Yamagiwa U.S.A.

Recalling a Japanese rice-paper screen, the shade of this lamp hangs from a cantilevered arm. The base and the bottom and top openings form a series of squares that complement the shade's hipped form, mirroring Wright's roofs. A floor lamp is also available.

Wright Picture Frames
(below left)
Dana-Thomas House, 1902
Alder in a walnut finish
4" by 6" or 3" square opening
Nos. 46616, 46615
MoMA Design Store

Art glass windows in a number of Wright houses were the inspiration for a series of picture frames. In addition to this prairie sumac motif, other designs are derived from the Winslow house (cast zinc alloy frame), Coonley playhouse (enameled frame), and Ennis house (walnut-finished alder frame)

Johnson Wax Desk and Chair
(above)
Johnson Wax Administration Building, 1936
Metal frame in red or black with wood tops and arms
39" high, 84¼" wide, 32" deep (desk)
34½" high, 24" wide, 21¼" deep (chair)
Leather or fabric upholstery
Nos. 617, 618
Cassina USA

The office furniture revolution that Wright began in 1903 with his Larkin Administration Building was won in 1936 with his design for the Johnson Wax Administration Building in Racine, Wisconsin. As they have since the building opened in 1939, employees still sit at desks and on chairs whose sinuous lines harmonize with the building itself. Tubular steel was chosen for efficiency, the red color to coordinate with the exterior's red brick. The set swirls with circular forms, from the desk drawers to the seat, back, and base of the four-legged chair on casters (originally three legged). Three parallel desktops in wood float above the desk, which includes two drawers, a hanging wastebasket, and file racks. The red metal version is topped with cherry, while the black set uses black-stained ash for the desktops.

Boulder Bookends
(below right)
Frank Lloyd Wright Home and Studio, 1898
Cast plaster, tinted red
8" high, 5½" square
Nicholas Bros. Stoneworks

A pair of these crouching figures, representing mankind struggling to transcend earthly bounds, sit on piers to announce the entrance to Wright's Oak Park studio. Created originally in collaboration with the sculptor Richard Bock, the expressive granite figures have also been reproduced as a large outdoor sculpture and a smaller paperweight.

Robie Brass Wall Sconce
Robie House, 1908
Antique brass and frosted glass
7⅛" high, 8⅞" wide, 11" deep
No. B2326
Yamagiwa U.S.A.

Mimicking moonlight, a half-moon globe is suspended from a top plate perforated with abstract fern designs visible above and below.

Robie Wood Wall Sconce
Robie House, 1908
Cherry and frosted glass
7" high, 11¼" wide, 13⅛" deep
No. B2324
Yamagiwa U.S.A.

A globe of soft light seems to float out from the wall, held in place only by a square band of wood encircling it at midpoint.

Sumac Wall Sconce
Dana-Thomas House, 1902
Polished brass and iridescent glass
13⅜" high, 3¾" wide, 5" deep
No. B2498
Yamagiwa U.S.A.

Iridescent glass in this sconce complements windows throughout the Dana house, Wright's most elaborate essay in stylized art glass.

Sumac Table Lamp
Dana-Thomas House, 1902
Polished brass and iridescent glass
10½" high, 4⅞" square
No. B2298
Yamagiwa U.S.A.

Wright's rectilinear patterns in glass such as this were designed to be more easily fabricated than medieval stained glass.

Taliesin Wood Floor Lamp
Taliesin, 1925
Cherry
80⅛" high, 16⅛" square
No. S2308
Yamagiwa U.S.A.

When he needed lights for his study and Hillside Theater at Taliesin, Wright adapted a Midway Gardens light using square boxes.

Taliesin Wood Table Lamp
Taliesin, 1925
Cherry
29¾" high, 8¼" square
No. S2310
Yamagiwa U.S.A.

Glass-less boxes fashioned of delicate wood and positioned around a spine project soft, indirect light filled with mystery.

Taliesin Wood 7-Lamp Pendant
Taliesin, 1932
Cherry
5'5¾" high, 16½" wide, 8" deep
No. P2430
Yamagiwa U.S.A.

In the pendant versions of Wright's wood lamp, the boxes holding the light bulbs are placed at 180-degree angles to the central pole.

Taliesin Wood 11-Lamp Pendant
Taliesin, 1932
Cherry
7'4¾" high, 16½" wide, 8" deep
No. P2428
Yamagiwa U.S.A.

Reflecting shades increase the intensity of the light output. Even unlighted, the Taliesin lamps are pure Wrightian sculpture.

Umbrella Sumac Lamp
Dana-Thomas House, 1902
Brass and iridescent glass
22⅝" high, 27¾" square
No. S2296
Yamagiwa U.S.A.

Based on an original lamp in the
Dana-Thomas house, the shade of
this single-pedestal lamp fans out in
sixteen panels recalling the prairie
sumac that sets the residence's
decorative theme. This and the
double-pedestal lamp pictured
below rest on solid square feet.

Double-Pedestal Lamp *(below right)*
Dana-Thomas House, 1902
Brass and iridescent glass
23¼" high, 32½" wide, 19¼" deep
No. S2298
Yamagiwa U.S.A.

Stylized leaves of prairie sumac
are recreated in iridescent glass
on the lamp's shade—hipped
and broad like the roof of one
of Wright's Prairie houses.
Beneath the shade, a pair of panels
mimics walls to complete the
analogy of a perfect house.

Butterfly Chandelier *(above)*
Dana-Thomas House, 1902
Brass and iridescent glass
22" high, 23¼" square
No. P2230
Yamagiwa U.S.A.

Recalling fluttering butterflies on
the prairie, four pendants like these
light the dining table at the Dana-
Thomas house and another hangs
in the stair landing near the gallery.
All relate to the "butterfly" art
glass transom over the front door.
The composition, an unusually
complex interweaving of planes in
glass and brass, reinforces the
sumac motif of the house's
spectacular art glass and lighting.

Storer Torchère *(right)*
Storer House, 1923
Painted steel and frosted glass
6' 4" high, 6⅛" wide, 8" deep
No. S2304
Yamagiwa U.S.A.

The square light as well as a
matching sconce pick up the shapes
of the concrete blocks and the
steel rods used in the house, one
of Wright's textile block designs.
Intersecting rectangles framing the
globe mirror the inset squares
forming the base. The entire design
reflects a modernity characteristic
of the Art Deco style. To increase
light in the Storer house, Wright
also devised a glassed variant of the
textile block that was perforated
and lighted from behind.

Eucalyptus Window
and Door Panels
Ennis House, 1923
Handcrafted glass
Various sizes
Art Glass Collection
Andersen Windows

Four panels inspired by Wright designs are available for insertion into Andersen windows and patio doors, allowing homeowners to experience full-size art glass windows as he envisioned them. The Eucalyptus pattern recalls the stylized plant motif used in the Ennis house, the last of the architect's homes to include art glass. Also available are Colonnade, adapted from Unity Temple (1905); Prairie Rhythm, inspired by the Coonley house (1907); and Wichita, based on windows in the Allen house (1917) in Wichita, Kansas.

Coonley Playhouse Clerestory 1
(below)
Coonley Playhouse, 1912
Clear and flashed opal glass in solid zinc-channel construction
17⅞" high, 33¾" wide
Oakbrook-Esser Studios

Balloons and circular motifs had begun to fascinate Wright long before he received the commission to create a kindergarten for his previous clients the Avery Coonleys. In a structure designed

for progressive education, he was able to stretch his sense of playfulness. Wright's most famous creation here is a window triptych transferring to glass the fun of a parade complete with balloons, a flag, and stylized square confetti (above). But even the school's high clerestory windows pick up the beat, marching around the building in vibrant primary colors and orange to complete the joy of a holiday parade captured in glass.

Coonley Playhouse Triptych Shade
Coonley Playhouse, 1912
Various fabrics
Custom printing up to 15' square
Electronic operation optional
No. SV-FLW-BLN
Lutron Electronics

For those who want to recreate the effect of Wright's art glass windows without using glass, two of his most famous windows have been transformed into translucent shades. The lively design shown—capturing the all-American spirit of a parade—features the left and right panels of the architect's Coonley playhouse triptych window. Here joyful elements of an American parade are reduced to pure abstraction. Also available are versions of Wright's Tree of Life windows for the Darwin Martin house (1904) in Buffalo, New York.

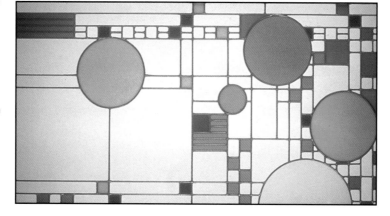

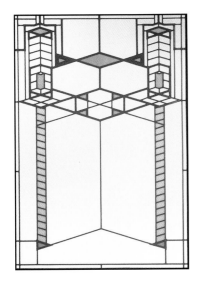

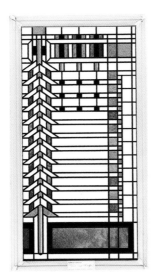

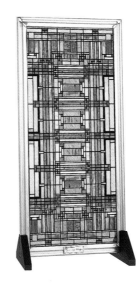

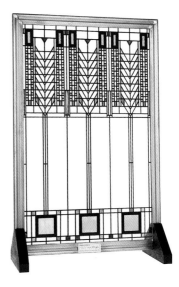

Robie Window I
Robie House, 1908
Clear and colored iridescent glass in solid copper-channel construction
43⅞" high, 15½" wide
Oakbrook-Esser Studios

The windows in this Prairie house in Chicago are one of its best architectural features. Screening the view and dressed in the prairie's autumnal hues, the diamond shapes derive from the house's own roof.

May Basket Glass Ornament *(below)*
Liberty Magazine, 1926–27
Iridescent glass
12⅛" square
No. 9055
Glassmasters

Although highly stylized, Wright's suggested *Liberty* magazine cover design for May conveys the lushness and optimism of spring.

Darwin Martin Window Ornament
Darwin Martin House, 1904
Iridescent glass
11¼" high, 6¼" wide
No. 8067
Glassmasters

Small casement windows in the house's living room feature a chevron floral pattern reminiscent of the sumac windows in the Dana-Thomas house. The colors and geometric motifs complement the Martin house's famous Tree of Life windows while creating their own unique vision of nature. Wright's plan was to use complex chevron patterns in the upstairs windows and simpler, more rectilinear designs on the first floor. However, the appearance of chevron-based "foliage" downstairs provides continuity in the overall treatment of the house's windows.

Oak Park Skylight Ornament
Frank Lloyd Wright Home and Studio, 1898
Iridescent glass
13⅜" high, 6⅜" wide
No. 8064
Glassmasters

With this green-and-gold skylight, Wright created the effect of an autumn forest in his new studio.

Dana Butterfly Glass Ornament *(below)*
Dana-Thomas House, 1902
Iridescent glass
5½" high, 19⅛" wide
No. 9040
Glassmasters

Semicircular transoms filled with colorful art glass butterflies greet visitors to this grand Prairie house. Their wings emerge from overlapping triangles holding bars filled with muted autumn coloration.

Tree of Life Glass Ornament
Darwin Martin House, 1904
Iridescent glass
12⅞" high, 8½" wide
No. 8026
Glassmasters

This geometric rendition giving the illusion of three trees in bloom appears in banks of windows under the roofline and elsewhere in the house, renowned for the amount and complexity of its art glass.

Opalescent Ornament *(below)*
Darwin Martin House, 1904
Iridescent glass
8⅞" square
No. 9099
Glassmasters

Intricate opalescent skylights such as this brought soft light into the interior of the Martin house, making it seem an indoor garden and thus bringing it close to nature.

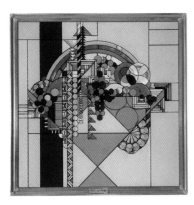

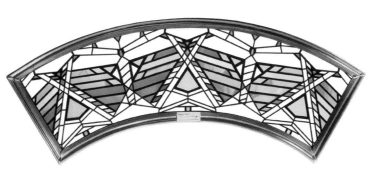

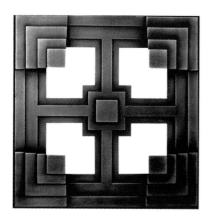

Storer House Block
Storer House, 1923
Cast aluminum with a copper-plated and patinated finish
16" square
Historical Arts and Casting

One of the four textile block houses Wright designed in the Los Angeles area in the 1920s, the Storer house combines a variety of block patterns to create a lacy fabric woven of concrete. Solid blocks are mixed with perforated ones to allow light to shine through and shadows to add mystery throughout the house. This metal reproduction featuring cascading squares is based on the block motif used for room dividers and curtain walls in the bedrooms.

Round and Square Fruit Bowls
Schwartz House, 1939
Bronze
4" high, 10" wide
Historical Arts and Casting

For the Schwartz house, a Usonian design in Two Rivers, Wisconsin, Wright's attention to detail extended even to where the owners would display their fruit.

Two dramatic bowls, one round and the other square, were designed but only the round version was made at the time. Minimalist in their varying geometric forms, the decorative pieces use the simplest of solids and voids to etch their shapes in space; triangular legs hold them aloft. These half-scale reproduction bowls were created from Wright's drawings.

Four-Square Vase
Heritage-Henredon Furniture Company, 1955
8" square (bronze)
4" square (half scale in pewter)
Historical Arts and Casting

As part of a line of furniture created in 1955 for the Heritage-Henredon Furniture Company, Wright also designed several vases intended to complement the furniture's rectilinear shapes. He was never a fan of mass-produced furnishings—believing that they should grow organically from the individual design of each house—yet he undertook the Taliesin Line to make his ideas available to a wider audience. This vase built around inset squares uses the same geometric motif Wright chose for his own red-tile signature block.

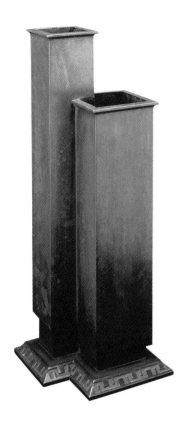

Duo Vase
Heritage-Henredon Furniture
Company, 1955
Bronze
21" high, 7½" wide
Historical Arts and Casting

To accompany his small Four-Square Vase, Wright in 1955 also designed two tall vases perfect for the wildflowers and dried weeds he liked to display at home. The Duo Vase offers two vessels in one, with varying heights for better display. A Greek key pattern like one used on the furniture runs around the base.

Tall Square Vase
Heritage-Henredon Furniture
Company, 1955
Bronze
16½" high, 3" square
Historical Arts and Casting

The Tall Square Vase elongates Wright's favorite square form to receive a carefully arranged bouquet. Ornament comes from the contrasting bands forming the lip and the base. Prototypes for all the 1955 vases, made by Minic in olive wood with copper liners, were shown with the furnishings line in the November 1955 *House Beautiful,* but they were never available to the public until recently.

Copper Urn
circa 1898
18" or 9" (copper)
4½" (quarter scale in pewter)
Historical Arts and Casting

At least nine of these eminently geometric urns are known to have been made for select Wright clients—the Wallers, Susan Lawrence Dana, the Coonleys, and Browne's Bookstore, among others—as well as for the architect himself; one graced his home and studio in Oak Park. The accessory stars in many contemporaneous photographs of his commissions. With its sinuous forms tracing the urn's rotundity, the container shows Wright's debt to his mentor, Louis Sullivan, and was one of his favorite objects, appearing with minor variations during his career. Writing later, Wright reminisced that he "fell in love with sheet copper as a building material." Its robust autumnal hue perfectly fit the architect's prairie palette.

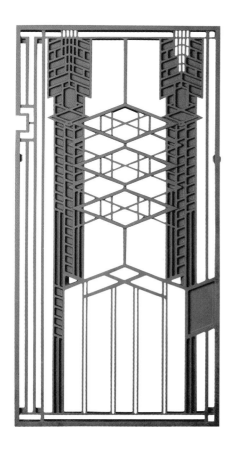

Robie Gate
Robie House, 1908
Painted aluminum
31" high, 16½" wide
Historical Arts and Casting

Wright's world-famous Robie house in Chicago, acknowledging the twentieth century's quick adoption of the automobile, included a large garage skillfully tucked into the front of the house. This gate, adapted from one in the motor court, echoes the residence's noted art glass windows—some of the most spectacular of the architect's Prairie period. Like the windows, the design's angular lines recall stalks of grain but derive from the house's roofline.

Votive Candles
Glass and bronze
3⁷⁄₁₆" or 6³⁄₁₆" or 7⅝" high,
4" square
Historical Arts and Casting

These short, medium, and tall glass-and-bronze votives are modern adaptations featuring typical Wrightian art glass and graphic design patterns. Patterns first used for windows in some of his houses as well as on the title page of his book *The House Beautiful* (1896) have been reinterpreted to create these decorative lights with interchangeable brass panels.

Candlestick Vase *(top)*
1902
Bronze
7" high, 3" square
Historical Arts and Casting

Angled upward to emulate a skyscraper, this little vase doubling as a candlestick is one of several Wright floral containers with similar lofty aspirations. The reproduction is based on a Wright drawing, but the design was probably never made at the time. It is available in two finishes and comes with a glass vial for flowers and a bobeche to catch candle wax.

Pocket Vase
1902
Bronze
18" high, 8" square
Historical Arts and Casting

As in other designs, Wright used concentrically rotated squares here to brilliant effect. He designed this gem of a vase at the request of James A. Miller and Brother of Chicago, artisans who executed a number of the architect's decorative pieces. The rotating squares produce smaller secondary openings that surround the main vertical element. Cascading triangles add a geometric counterpoint.

Darwin Martin House Vase
Darwin Martin House, 1904
Bronze
30½" high
Historical Arts and Casting

This unusual tall, tapered vase appeared in a drawing for a book-shelf in the Darwin Martin house in Buffalo, New York, although it is not certain if it was actually made for the Martins. Famous for its Tree of Life windows, the Martin house was filled with nature motifs, from a glass-mosaic fireplace to a conservatory and a pergola, all lost over the years. Wright would also have wanted his clients to be sur-rounded with natural bouquets in perfect containers such as this.

Darwin Martin House Candle Planter
Darwin Martin House, 1904
Oak or cherry with bronze
29" high, 10" square
Historical Arts and Casting

Following his goal of making the dining table and chairs a "room within a room," Wright often built elaborate lighting devices into the table itself during his Prairie years. For the Martin house he devised a unique combination planter and candleholder. It joins a circle and a square—favorite geometric forms—to hold the planter bowl, now available in blown glass or spun copper. The base itself is available in oak or cherry. The four bronze candlesticks have movable shades made of glass or copper.

Duo Flower Stand
1902
Bronze
26" high, 5⅝" wide
Historical Arts and Casting

This two-in-one vase design, also created at the request of James A. Miller and Brother, most likely was never manufactured. With its playful conjoining of geometric shapes, it may have served as a pre-cursor of Wright's later double vase designed in 1955 to accom-pany his home furnishings line.

Weed Holder
circa 1895
Copper
29" high
Historical Arts and Casting

Because Wright liked to display dried natural flowers at home, he designed this sinuous four-sided vase and used it in his own studio. Set on a pyramidal base, the vase's attenuated shape hints at the mile-high skyscraper Wright proposed for Chicago in 1954. The object became a favorite decorative acces-sory, one he also bestowed on clients. A 14½-inch half-scale version is available in pewter.

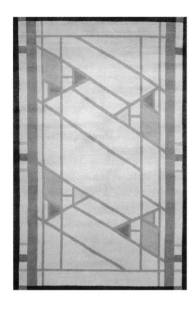
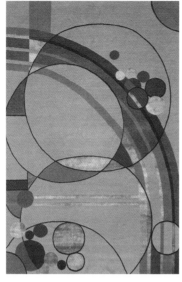
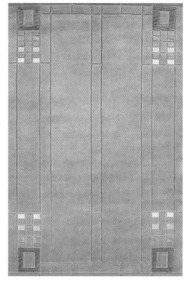
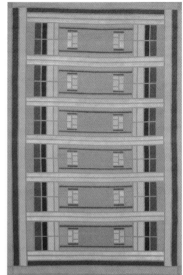

California Romanza Rug
Hollyhock House, 1917
60-knot wool
4' by 6' to 10' by 14'
Custom colors and sizes
No. FLW 6001
Costikyan Carpets/Alamadia

Some of Wright's most abstract windows—in Aline Barnsdall's Hollywood home—provided inspiration for this rug. Triangles dance along art glass throughout the house to evoke hollyhocks, the owner's favorite flower. Most unusual was the purple coloration.

Liberty Balloons Rug
Liberty Magazine, 1926–27
100-knot wool and silk
4' by 6' to 10' by 14'
Custom colors and sizes
Nos. FLW S004MU, 6S004NA
Costikyan Carpets/Alamadia

Based on one of the most-loved designs from Wright's *Liberty* magazine series, this rug displays a joyous concatenation of large and small circles intersecting with segments of circles. Wright later used this vibrant concept as the basis of plans for his houses.

Darwin D. Martin Rug
Darwin Martin House, 1904
60-knot wool and silk
4' by 6' to 10' by 14'
Custom colors and sizes
No. FLW 68GL
Costikyan Carpets/Alamadia

"T" shapes such as the motif in this rug can be found in both the dining room and the living room of this noted Prairie house in Buffalo, New York. The perfectly symmetrical corner designs were inspired by the birdhouse as well as an oak table design in the Martin house.

Oak Park Skylight Rug
Frank Lloyd Wright Home and Studio, 1898
60-knot wool and silk
4' by 6' to 10' by 14'
Custom colors and sizes
No. FLW S003
Costikyan Carpets/Alamadia

Based on a skylight in Wright's studio featuring golden prairie colors, each pane in this rug is separated by a triple line of wool to emulate the thin metal dividers found in the original art glass composition.

Coonley II Rug *(left)*
Coonley Playhouse, 1912
60-knot wool
4' by 6' to 10' by 14'
Custom colors and sizes
No. FLW 6005
Costikyan Carpets/Alamadia

The circles that cavort in the triptych and clerestory windows of this kindergarten have been translated into a quiet pattern for the floor. Unlike the primary colors of the original, the rug's palette uses nature-inspired tones: sea green, sky blue, soft beige, and taupes.

May House Rug *(right)*
May House, 1908
Handtufted wool
Custom design
PWV Studios

This carpet, using squares and abstracted leaf motifs repeated throughout the house, is one of the reproductions made exclusively for the May house (pages 82–83) when it was restored. Wright often used similar chevrons as stand-ins for natural foliage. Not for sale, the rug is an example of the artisans' work in replicating historic documents.

Maple Leaf Rug
Handtufted wool
Custom sizes
Schumacher/Patterson, Flynn
and Martin

In 1955 Schumacher pioneered a
commercial line of products based
on Wright designs, although no
carpets were among its original
offerings. This two-tone custom
rug is part of the firm's most
recent Wright collection, featuring
abstracted botanical designs. Japan-
esque in style, the rug displays an
intricate design of autumnal foliage
that can be customized to individual color and size specifications.

Prairie Foliage Fabric
Waterfall Stripe Fabric
Prairie Sumac Fabric
Various materials and colorways
Nos. 25363, 60151, 25357
Schumacher

These upholstered seats show off
several of Schumacher's Wright
fabrics featuring abstracted nature
motifs: grasses, vines, ferns, prairie
sumac, wisteria, pine bark, and
even waterfalls. Prairie Foliage is a
modified herringbone, Waterfall
Stripe comes from a Japanese
mulberry paper stencil, and Prairie
Sumac interprets a famous window
design from the Dana house.

Trellised Vine Fabric
Willits Glass Fabric
Masselink Ferns Fabric
Fern Meadow Fabric
Various materials and colorways
Nos. 25335, 20012, 12271, 25341
Schumacher

Trellised Vine, another interpretation from the Dana house, juxta-
poses vines with a rectilinear trellis
pattern. Willits Glass offers a herringbone weave of grasses based on
a skylight. Masselink Ferns derives
from a Japanese stencil in Wright's
own collection. Fern Meadow
reproduces a screen by Wright's
close associate Eugene Masselink.

Fern Stencil Wallpaper
Bougainvillea Wallpaper
Incense Wallpaper
Nos. 525266, 525304, 525314
Schumacher

Earth-tone colors predominate in
the Schumacher collection. Fern
Stencil was inspired by an intricate
mulberry paper stencil in Wright's
personal collection of Japanese
images. Bougainvillea recognizes
several glass mosaic fireplace
murals in a wisteria pattern.
Incense, which was released in 1955
as a Schumacher fabric, may have
been based on a mazelike Japanese
game board named Genji-Ko.

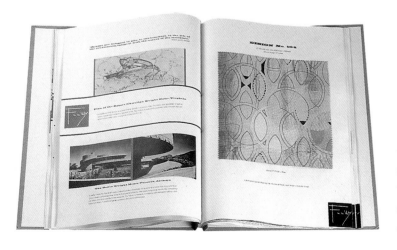

In 1955 Wright designed a collection of fabrics and wall coverings
for Schumacher that was called the
Taliesin Line. The catalogue's cover
and pages feature Wright's square
signature block in Cherokee red.

Imperial Hotel China (above left)
Imperial Hotel, 1922
Porcelain with 22-karat gold edge
No. IM/Set 5
WrightStyle

The formal china that Wright designed for the main dining room of his famous Imperial Hotel in Tokyo was rimmed in a golden checkerboard pattern borrowed from the room's windows. The five-piece place setting can be supplemented with other pieces, including a soup bowl, platter, serving bowl, teapot, sugar and creamer, and espresso cup and saucer.

Imperial Hotel Mug
(below left)
Imperial Hotel, 1922
Porcelain with 22-karat gold edge
No. IM/Mug
WrightStyle

A new coffee mug, featuring a gold handle that complements the 22-karat decoration, has been added to the Imperial Hotel dinnerware. Within the rim is a series of crosses built of squares, while a short pendant motif recalls the building's architecture. This motif was reinterpreted on the hotel's set of simpler room-service china.

Cabaret Dinnerware Mug
(below right)
Imperial Hotel, 1922–33
Porcelain
12 oz. capacity
No. CAB/Mug4
WrightStyle

For the Imperial Hotel's more informal Cabaret Dining Room, Wright designed one of his most beloved decorative accessories: dinnerware bearing a colorful array of circles in red, yellow, green, and blue that float around like champagne bubbles. This breakfast or dessert mug is a modern adaptation.

Cabaret Dinnerware Plate
(above right)
Imperial Hotel, 1922–33
Porcelain
8" diameter
No. CAB/PL4
WrightStyle

A matching plate bears the same joyous pattern as the mug, both continuing Wright's playful use of circular motifs that began when he brought balloons home to his children in Oak Park. He continued this theme in windows for the Coonley playhouse (1912) and in murals at Midway Gardens (1913).

Guggenheim Tableware *(above)*
Guggenheim Museum, 1943–59
Porcelain
No. GU
WrightStyle

The spiraling ziggurat design of Wright's famed Guggenheim Museum in New York City inspired this new set of tableware. Pieces range from a covered biscotti jar as white and rotund as its architectural model to a teapot with a sugar bowl and creamer to a salt and pepper set. For coffee drinkers there is a mug as well as sets of cappuccino and espresso cups and saucers.

Wright Crystal Candlesticks *(top right)*
Leerdam Glassfabrik Company, 1930
Lead crystal
3½" or 6" or 8½" high
Nos. 7500-2110, 2111, 2112
Reed and Barton

Wright Crystal Vase, Bowl, and Picture Frame *(bottom right)*
Leerdam Glassfabrik Company, 1930
Lead crystal
9¾" vase, 10" bowl, 6" frame
Nos. 7500-2113, 2114, 2115
Reed and Barton

In the late 1920s Wright was asked by a Dutch glassmaker to create a line of tabletop items for commercial production. Only one, a flower vase, was ever produced because glassmaking techniques had not caught up to Wright's vision. Now a number of these futuristic designs have been adapted for contemporary use. All feature an architectonic hexagonal design that transforms them into faceted jewels.

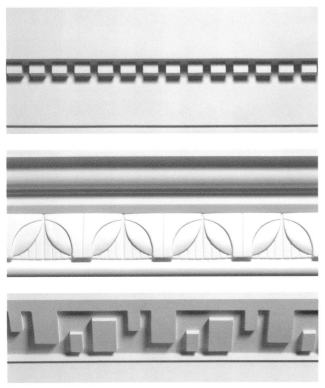

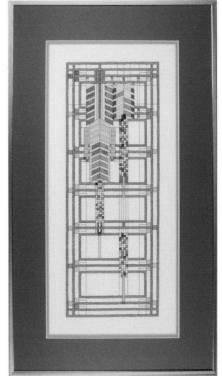

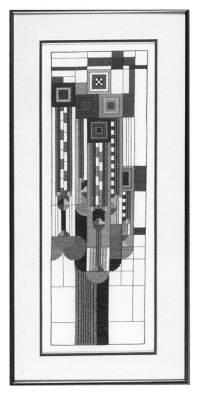

Architectural Moulding
Darwin Martin House, 1904 *(top)*
Polymer
8" high, 12' wide, 2⁷⁄₁₆" deep
No. 19510
Focal Point Architectural Products

A number of architectural mouldings have been developed based on Wright motifs. The first one shown replicates dentilwork on frieze boards in the Martin house.

Architectural Moulding
David Wright House, 1950 *(center)*
Polymer
7¾" high, 12' wide, 3" deep
No. 19500
Focal Point Architectural Products

The spiraling, circular desert house the architect designed for his son David Wright inspired another moulding pattern. This one recreates an edging motif of entwined circles stamped into the house's concrete blocks. Other mouldings are adapted from Wright's home in Oak Park, Midway Gardens, as well as the Moore, May, and Price residences.

Architectural Moulding
Heritage-Henredon Furniture, 1955
(bottom)
Polymer
5¾" high, 12' wide, 4¼" deep
No. 19540
Focal Point Architectural Products

An unusual moulding pattern was created from ornamental details on furniture designed for Wright's Taliesin Line, which was released by Heritage-Henredon in 1955.

Usonian Doormat *(below right)*
Pope-Leighey House, 1939
Natural and bleached woven coir
18" high, 30" wide
No. DM/FLW911
WrightStyle

One of several doormats featuring Wright designs, this one reproduces perforated-wood windows in the children's room of the Pope-Leighey house in Virginia, an early Usonian residence. To spare owners the expense of art glass windows, the architect turned to geometric wood cutouts in his later houses to create similar effects.

Fountain Cross-stitch Kit
Dana-Thomas House, 1902
Kit with evenweave fabric
17" by 6"
(23" by 13" wide if framed)
No. 833
Heartland House Designs

Variations of this abstract sumac motif are used on art glass doors and windows in the Prairie Style house, including a wall of glass framing a fountain in the reception room. In it, rows of chevrons bloom above a checkerboard-like trellis to heighten geometric contrasts. Other needlework kits feature additional Wright designs.

Saguaro Forms Cross-stitch Kit
Liberty Magazine, 1926–27
Kit with evenweave fabric
16½" by 5½"
(22½" by 11½" if framed)
No. 194
Heartland House Designs

One of the twelve cover designs Wright created for *Liberty* magazine featured this lively abstraction of the Arizona desert's saguaro cactus—one element in the new design vocabulary Wright developed in the late 1920s. Never published, it reappeared as a glass mural by Eugene Masselink in the Arizona Biltmore Hotel (1927, Albert McArthur).

Fretwork Panels
Blossom House, 1892 *(top)*
American Luxfer Prism Company,
1897 *(bottom)*
Solid brass with hand patina finish
Black lacquer frame and glass
12½" square
Nos. WA001/004, 009
WrightStyle

A number of Wright's geometric
patterns have been transferred to
brass and framed for hanging. The
Blossom design is adapted from the
entry sidelight, while the Luxfer
pattern comes from a patented
system of glass blocks Wright
designed; it features a Sullivanesque
swirl of ellipses over a circle inside
a square. Floating in their frames,
these fretwork panels recreate the
original three-dimensional effect.

California Block House Bookends
(above)
Community Playhouse, 1921
Sandstone
6½" high, 7" square
No. FLWPB
Nichols Bros. Stoneworks

Using concrete block patterns
from Wright's four California
textile block houses and his unbuilt
"Little Dipper" Community Playhouse, five bookend sets have been
created. Wright designed perfora-
tions in the blocks to let light
through. The series also includes
Millard, Freeman, Storer, and Ennis
house textile block bookends. For
each, the square block is sliced in
half to form a triangular bookend.

California Block House Lanterns
(below)
Textile Block Houses, 1923
Cast stone
5" high, 5¾" square
Nos. FLWWML, FLWEL, FLWSL,
FLWFL, FLWPL, FLWCBL
Nichols Bros. Stoneworks

Like the bookends, these tabletop
lanterns reproduce five of Wright's
perforated concrete block patterns
developed in California in the
1920s. From left to right are the
Ennis, Community Playhouse,
Millard, Storer, and Freeman
patterns. A sixth combination
lantern uses a different pattern
on each of the four sides. Designed
for indoor or outdoor use, the
lanterns include a candle.

Pinnacle Vase
Leerdam Glassfabrik Company,
1930
High-fired stoneware
16" high
No. CV/002
WrightStyle

Inspired by the hexagonal and octagonal patterns Wright saw in daylilies
at Taliesin, this vase was originally
drawn in 1930 as part of his glassware collection for the Dutch glass
company Leerdam. Now the vessel,
like several original Wright vases,
has been manufacturered in the
natural green stoneware favored by
many potters during the Arts and
Crafts movement. For the Dana
house hearth, the architect created
a green Teco vase—square at the
bottom, rising to an octagonal lip—
ornamented with sumac motifs.

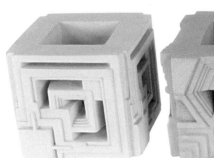

Allen House Urn *(above left)*
Allen House, 1917
Cast sandstone
27½" or 41¼" or 55" wide
Nos. NFLWASA, NFLWAMA,
NFLWALA
Nichols Bros. Stoneworks

A late Prairie Style design, the residence Wright designed for Governor Henry J. Allen of Kansas turns inward around a central landscaped courtyard. Near its reflecting pond sits this massive spherical urn, 55 inches in diameter.

Oak Park Studio Urn *(below left)*
Frank Lloyd Wright Home and
Studio, 1898
Cast sandstone
24" or 35¾" or 45" wide
Nos. NFLWSS, NFLWSM,
NFLWSL
Nichols Bros. Stoneworks

Outside his studio, added alongside the Oak Park house in 1898, Wright displayed a highly geometric planter. Using a circle-in-a-square motif, he cantilevered the lip over the base—as he would begin to do with his houses.

Oak Park Residence Urn *(above)*
Frank Lloyd Wright Home and
Studio, 1889
Cast sandstone
20" or 28½" or 37" wide
Nos. NFLWHS, NFLWHM,
NFLWHL
Nichols Bros. Stoneworks

Wright used planters to draw nature close to the house. For his own Oak Park home, the young architect designed this classic urn to flank the entry stairs. The medium-sized replica is made to the full scale of the original.

American System Built Urn
(below center)
American System Built Houses,
1915–17
Cast sandstone
35" high, 24" diameter
No. NFLWASBH
Nichols Bros. Stoneworks

Seeking ways of making homes more affordable, Wright developed a system of prefabricated houses for Arthur Richards of Milwaukee. This optional accompanying vase has since been made for the Wynant house (1917) in Gary, Indiana.

Robie House Urn *(above right)*
Robie House, 1908
Cast sandstone
30" or 45" or 60" wide
Nos. NFLWRS, NFLWRM,
NFLWRL
Nichols Bros. Stoneworks

Hugging the ground, with a dramatically cantilevered lip, this famous planter conveys the earth-loving spirit of the Robie house itself. The large size is a full-scale version of the original urn outside the Chicago landmark, Wright's most famous Prairie residence.

Westcott House Urn *(below right)*
Westcott House, 1907
Cast sandstone
20½" or 34" or 48" wide
Nos. NFLWWS, NFLWWM,
NFLWWL
Nichols Bros. Stoneworks

The planters announcing this Prairie Style house in Springfield, Ohio, grew to truly heroic proportions: 7 feet high. Reflecting shapes used in the urns outside his own studio, albeit with a smaller base, they put nature on public display.

Nakoma Statue *(above left)*
Nakoma Country Club, 1923–24
Cast sandstone
24" or 36" high
Nos. FLWNAS, FLWNA
Nichols Bros. Stoneworks

Nakomis Statue *(above center)*
Nakoma Country Club, 1923–24
Cast sandstone
36" or 54" high
Nos. FLWNSS, FLWNS
Nichols Bros. Stoneworks

Wright's tentlike design for the Nakoma Country Club in Madison, Wisconsin, was not realized until recently, when the clubhouse was constructed under the supervision of Taliesin Architects. Included among Wright's drawings for the club were these sculptural figures paying tribute to the state's Winnebago Indians: the female Nakoma and the headdress-bedecked Nakomis. The beaded Nakoma and a child carry bowls as round as their own heads, while Nakomis instructs a young Indian boy. The larger versions of each figure are suitable for outdoor use.

Garden Sprite *(above)*
Midway Gardens, 1913
Cast concrete
31" high, 7" wide, 6" deep
Pedestal: 11" high, 11" wide, 8½" deep
Nos. FLWS, FLWSP
Nichols Bros. Stoneworks

Garden Sprite with Baton
(above right)
Midway Gardens, 1913
Cast concrete
31" high, 7" wide, 6" deep
Pedestal: 11" high, 11" wide, 8½" deep
Nos. FLWSPB, FLWSP
Nichols Bros. Stoneworks

In the heart of industrial Chicago, Midway Gardens (razed in 1929) was a magical entertainment complex that integrated the visual and performing arts with distinctive Wrightian architecture. Some of its most memorable icons were the expressively geometric sprites designed by the sculptor Alfonso Ianelli under Wright's direction. Against a backdrop of yellow brick and cast-concrete walls, they marched around the sunken garden to add a touch of humanity to the architecture. Full-scale replicas are 66 and 64 inches high. For indoor display, 12-inch-high tabletop sprites are also available.

Moore House Stepping Stone
or Plaque *(below)*
Moore House, 1895, 1923
Cast stone
10" square, 1" deep
No. FLWNM
Nichols Bros. Stoneworks

For this early house on a large
corner lot not far from his Oak
Park home, Wright gave his clients
what they wanted: an Elizabethan-
style home. After a fire in 1922 he
modernized a number of features.
This stylized floral motif comes
from a wood-fret doorway that
recalls ceiling lights installed in
Wright's dining room and the
upstairs playroom for his children.

Larkin Plaques *(right)*
Larkin Administration Building,
1903
Sandstone
5¾" high, 14" wide, ¾" deep
Nichols Bros. Stoneworks

Wright called his Larkin office
building in Buffalo, New York, "the
first emphatic protest in architecture." The entire structure, which
he saw as a "simple cliff of brick,"
looked inward to give company
employees a more pleasant environment than the one surrounding
the building. Light filled the central
space from a skylighted atrium
ringed by office "galleries." The
architect even designed innovative
metal furniture intended to ease
the sitters' posture and make the
evening cleanup more efficient.
A conservatory and flower boxes
brought nature indoors to com-
pensate for the lack of rewarding
scenery outdoors. And on the
atrium's fifth-floor level, Wright
inscribed homilies in stone to not-
so-subtly urge the employees of
this mail-order company to excel.
Five of these sayings have been
reproduced in stone plaques:
"Faith, Hope, Charity"; "Integrity,
Loyalty, Fidelity"; "Prudence,
Learning, Wisdom"; "Sincerity,
Humility, Courage"; and "Thought,
Feeling, Action." Each plaque replicates the lettering and geometric
motifs of the original panels, which
complemented the abstracted
capitals atop the atrium's columns.
This landmark was razed in 1950.

DECORATIVE ARTS SUPPLIERS

General Information

Frank Lloyd Wright Foundation
and Taliesin West Bookstore
12621 North Frank Lloyd Wright
Boulevard
Scottsdale, AZ 85259
T: +1 480-860-2700, ext. 221
F: +1 480-860-8472
www.franklloydwright.org
request@franklloydwright.org

Major Retail Outlets and Catalogues

Art Institute of Chicago
111 South Michigan Avenue
Chicago, IL 60603
T: +1 800-621-9337
F: +1 847-299-8286
www.artinstituteshop.org

Dana-Thomas House Foundation
Sumac Shop
301 East Lawrence Avenue
Springfield, IL 62703
T: +1 217-744-3598
F: +1 217-788-9450
www.dana-thomas.org

Frank Lloyd Wright
Preservation Trust
931 Chicago Avenue
Oak Park, IL 60302-2097
T: +1 877-848-3559
F: +1 708-848-2327
www.wrightcatalog.org

MoMA Design Store*
Museum of Modern Art
11 West 53rd Street
New York, NY 10019-5401
T: +1 800-447-6662
F: +1 610-431-3333
www.moma.org

Taliesin Bookstore
P.O. Box 399
5607 County Highway C
Spring Green, WI 53588
T: +1 877-588-7900
F: +1 608-588-7919
www.taliesinbookstore.com

Suppliers

Alimadia Gallery
502 Division Street
Northfield, MN 55057
T: +1 507-645-1651
F: +1 952-400-5606
www.alimadia.com

Andersen Windows*
Andersen House, Dallow Street
Burton-on-Trent
Staffordshire DE142PQ, England
T: +44 (0) 1283-511122
F: +44 (0) 1283-510863
www.blackmillwork.co.uk

Bulova*
One Bulova Avenue
Woodside, NY 11377-7874
T: +1 877-204-3868
F: +1 718-204-3372
www.bulova.com

Cassina S.p.A.*
Via Busnelli, 1
20036 Meda (MI), Italy
T: +1 39 (0) 362-3721
F: +1 39 (0) 362-342246
www.cassina.it

Cooper Art Glass*
405 Main Trail
Ormond Beach, FL 32174
T: +1 386-673-9990
F: +1 386-615-0094
www.cooperartglass.com
cooperartglass@earthlink.net

Costikyan Carpets*
1274 Springfield Avenue
New Providence, NJ 07974
T: +1 888-930-7847
F: +1 908-665-0020
www.costikyan.com
peter@costikyan.com

Focal Point Architectural Products*
3006 Anaconda Road
Tarboro, NC 27886
T: +1 800-662-5550
F: +1 800-352-9049
www.focalpointap.com
marketing@nomaco.com

Glassmasters*
2501 Mechanicsville Turnpike
Richmond, VA 23223
T: +1 800-488-2494
F: +1 804-648-7839
www.glassmasters.com

Heartland House Designs*
741 North Oak Park Avenue
Oak Park, IL 60302-1536
T: +1 708-383-2278
F: +1 708-383-2377
www.heartlandhouse.com

Historical Arts and Casting*
5580 West Bagley Park Road
West Jordan, UT 84088-5642
T: +1 800-225-1414
F: +1 801-280-2493
www.historicalarts.com
info@historicalarts.com

Peter Korab Studios
641 Belleforte Avenue
Oak Park, IL 60302
T: +1 708-383-3038

Lutron Electronics Company*
11520 Sun Shade Lane
Ashland, VA 23005
T: +1 800-446-1503
www.lutron.com

Nichols Bros. Stoneworks*
20209 Broadway
Snohomish, WA 98296
T: +1 800-483-5720
F: +1 425-483-5721
www.nicholsbros.com
info@nicholsbros.com

Oakbrook-Esser Studios*
129 East Wisconsin Avenue
Oconomowoc, WI 53066
T: +1 800-223-5193
F: +1 262-567-6487
www.oakbrookesser.com

PWV Studios
1735 Elizabeth Avenue, N.W.
Grand Rapids, MI 49501
T: +1 616-361-5659
F: +1 616-361-1090
pwvstudio@aol.com

Reed and Barton*
Miller Rogaska Crystal
144 West Britannia Street
Taunton, MA 02780-1643
T: +1 800-822-1824
F: +1 508-884-8864
www.reedbarton.com

F. Schumacher and Company*
79 Madison Avenue
New York, NY 1016
T: +1 800-523-1200 (information)
T: +1 212-213-7900 (showroom)
www.fschumacher.com

Swartzendruber Hardwood Creations
1100 Chicago Avenue
Goshen, IN 46528
T: +1 800-531-2502
F: +1 574-534-2504
www.swartzendruber.com
info@swartzendruber.com

Thos. Moser Cabinetmakers
415 Cumberland Avenue
Portland, ME 04101
T: +1 207-865-9148
F: +1 207-865-2879
www.thosmoser.com

WrightStyle*
10580 Newkirk Street, Suite 302
Dallas, TX 75220-2329
T: +1 877-858-0913
F: +1 972-409-0082
www.wrightstyle.com

Yamagiwa U.S.A. Corporation*
31340 Via Colinas, Unit 106
Westlake Village, CA 91362
T: +1 888-879-8611
F: +1 818-879-8640
www.yamagiwausa.com
yamagiwausa@aol.com

*Companies licensed by the
Frank Lloyd Wright Foundation;
a portion of the sales proceeds
benefits the Foundation's work.
Frank Lloyd Wright® is a federally
registered trademark owned by the
Frank Lloyd Wright Foundation.

ARCHITECTS AND DESIGNERS

The following design firms are represented in this book and continue to have active practices. Their projects are noted.

Bauhs Dring Seglin Main
One East Delaware Place
Suite 500
Chicago, IL 60611
T: +1 312-649-9484
www.bdsmarchitects.com

Frank Lloyd Wright home and studio (restoration chairman)

Arthur Dyson Architect
754 P Street
Suite C
Fresno, CA 93721
T: +1 559-486-3582
www.arthurdyson.com
adyson@att.net

Geringer house

Hasbrouck Peterson Zimoch Sirirattumrong
104 South Michigan Avenue
Suite 250
Chicago, IL 60603
T: +1 312-553-9600
www.hpzs.com
hpzs.@hpzs.com

Dana-Thomas house restoration

Maurice Jennings + David McKee, Architects
619 West Dickson Street
Fayetteville, AR 72701
T: +1 479-443-4742
www.jenningsmckeearch.com
jenningsmckee@arkansas.net

Edmondson house

Donald Kalec, Architect
5837 West Race Street
Chicago, IL 60644
T: +1 773-287-2773
dkalec@artic.edu

Frank Lloyd Wright home and studio (restoration director), Henderson house restoration

MacDonald and Mack Architects
712 Grain Exchange Building
Minneapolis, MN 55415
T: +1 612-341-4051
www.mmarchitd.com
info@mmarchitd.com

Purcell-Cutts house restoration

Milton Stricker Architect
3211 South Massachusetts Street
Seattle, WA 98144
T: +1 206-329-5277
strickerm@msn.com

Fisher house

Taliesin Architects
12621 North Frank Lloyd Wright Boulevard
Scottsdale, AZ 85259
T: +1 480-614-3500
www.taliesin-architects.com
clientservices@taliesin-architects.com

Benton house

John Garrett Thorpe, AIA
1033 South Boulevard
Oak Park, IL 60302
T: +1 708-386-1700
jgthorpe1@msn.com

Frank Lloyd Wright home and studio (restoration chairman)

Tilton, Kelly, and Bell
303 West Madison Street
Suite 1140
Chicago, IL 60606
T: +1 312-782-8333
www.tiltonkellybell.com
mbell@tiltonkellybell.com

Barr, Ingalls, May, and Zimmerman house restorations

Vinci/Hamp Architects
1147 West Ohio Street
Chicago, IL 60622
T: +1 312-733-7744
www.vinci-hamp.com
jvinci@vinci-hamp.com

Coonley playhouse restoration, Frank Lloyd Wright studio (restoration architect)

Eric Lloyd Wright
24680 Piuma Road
Malibu, CA 90265
T: +1 818-591-8992
studio@elwright.net

Auldbrass and Storer house restorations

FRANK LLOYD WRIGHT ORGANIZATIONS

For further information about Frank Lloyd Wright and his buildings, contact the following organizations as well as individual Wright sites listed on the opposite page.

Frank Lloyd Wright
Building Conservancy
5132 South Woodlawn Avenue
Chicago, IL 60615
T: +1 773-324-5600
www.savewright.org

Frank Lloyd Wright
Foundation
P.O. Box 4430
Scottsdale, AZ 85261-4430
T: +1 480-860-2700
www.franklloydwright.org

Frank Lloyd Wright
Preservation Trust
951 Chicago Avenue
Oak Park, IL 60302
T: +1 708-848-01976
www.wrightplus.org

WRIGHT SITES OPEN TO VISITORS

The following sites by Frank Lloyd Wright are open regularly or occasionally for visitation. Please call ahead to confirm availability, tour hours, and admission fees.

Affleck House
c/o College of Architecture
Lawrence Technological University
1925 North Woodward Avenue
Bloomfield Hills, MI 48013
T: +1 248-204-2880

Allen-Lambe House
255 North Roosevelt Avenue
Wichita, KS 67208
T: +1 316-687-1027
http://home.onemain.com/~allenlam/index.html

Barton House
118 Summit Avenue
Buffalo, NY 14214
T: +1 716-856-3858
www.darwinmartinhouse.org

Cheney House
Bed and Breakfast
520 North East Avenue
Oak Park, IL 60302
T: +1 708-524-2067
http://oakparknet.com

Dana-Thomas House
301 East Lawrence Avenue
Springfield, IL 62703
T: +1 217-782-6776
www.dana-thomas.org

Ennis-Brown House
2655 Glendower Avenue
Los Angeles, CA 90027-1114
T: +1 323-668-0234
www.ennisbrownhouse.org

Fallingwater
Route 381 South
Mill Run, PA 15464
T: +1 724-329-8501
www.wpconline.org/fallingwater-home.htm

Frank Lloyd Wright Home and Studio
951 Chicago Avenue
Oak Park, IL 60302
T: +1 708-848-1976
www.wrightplus.org

Freeman House
c/o University of Southern California
School of Architecture
1962 Glencoe Way
Los Angeles, CA 90068
T: +1 213-740-2723
www.usc.edu/dept/architecture/slide/Freeman

Gordon House
The Oregon Garden
879 West Main Street
Silverton, OR 97381
T: +1 503-874-6006
T: +1 877-674-2733, ext. 6006
www.oregongarden.org

Hanna House
c/o University Architect
655 Serra Street
Stanford, CA 94305
T: +1 650-723-7773

Hollyhock House
4808 Hollywood Boulevard
Los Angeles, CA 90027
T: +1 213-662-7272
www.hollyhockhouse.net

Edgar J. Kaufmann Office
Victoria and Albert Museum
Cromwell Road
South Kensington
London SW7 2RL, England
T: +1 20-7942-2000
www.vam.ac.uk

Kentuck Knob
P.O. Box 305
Chalk Hill, PA 15421
T: +1 724-329-1901
www.kentuck-knob.com

Little House II Library
Allentown Art Museum
Fifth and Court Streets
Allentown, PA 18105
T: +1 610-432-4333
www.allentownartmuseum.org

Little House II Living Room
Metropolitan Museum of Art
American Wing
Fifth Avenue at 82nd Street
New York, NY 10028
T: +1 212-879-5500, ext. 3791
www.metmuseum.org

Darwin Martin House
125 Jewett Parkway
Buffalo, NY 14214
T: +1 716-856-3858
www.darwinmartinhouse.org

May House
450 Madison Avenue, S.E.
Grand Rapids, MI 49503
T: +1 616-246-4821

Peterson Cottage
E9982 Fern Dell Road
Lake Delton, WI 53940
T: +1 608-254-6051 (tours)
T: +1 608-254-6551 (rentals)
www.sethpeterson.org

Pope-Leighey House
at Woodlawn Plantation
9000 Richmond Highway
Alexandria, VA 22309
T: +1 703-780-4000
www.nationaltrust.org

Robie House
5757 South Woodlawn Avenue
Chicago, IL 60637
T: +1 773-834-1847
www.robiehouse.org

Rosenbaum House
601 Riverview Drive
Florence, AL 35630
T: +1 256-740-8899
www.wrightinalabama.com
info@wrightinalabama.com

Stockman House
530 First Street, N.E.
Mason City, IA 50401
T: +1 641-423-1923
T: +1 641-421-3666
www.globegazette.com/sitepages/mktplace/flwstockman/flwstockman.htm

Taliesin
5607 County Highway C
at Highway 23
Spring Green, WI 53588
T: +1 877-588-7900
www.taliesinpreservation.org

Taliesin West
12621 North Frank Lloyd Wright Boulevard
Scottsdale, AZ 85259
T: +1 480-860-2700
www.franklloydwright.org

Walter House (Cedar Rock)
2611 Quasqueton Diag Boulevard
Quasqueton, IA 52326
T: +1 319-934-3572
www.state.ia.us/dnr/organiza/ppd/cedarock.htm

Zimmerman House
c/o Currier Museum of Art
201 Myrtle Way
Manchester, NH 03104
T: +1 603-669-6144
www.currier.org

FURTHER READING

Aguar, Charles E. and Berdeana. *Wrightscapes: Frank Lloyd Wright's Landscape Designs.* New York: McGraw-Hill, 2002.

Brooks, H. Allen. *The Prairie School.* Toronto: University of Toronto Press, 1972.

Hanks, David A. *The Decorative Designs of Frank Lloyd Wright.* 1979. Reprint, New York: Dover, 1999.

Hanna, Paul and Jean. *Frank Lloyd Wright's Hanna House: The Clients' Report.* Carbondale, Illinois: Southern Illinois University Press, 1981.

Hitchcock, Henry-Russell. *In the Nature of Materials: The Buildings of Frank Lloyd Wright, 1887–1941.* 1942. Reprint, New York: Da Capo, 1969.

Hoffmann, Donald. *Understanding Frank Lloyd Wright's Architecture.* New York: Dover, 1995.

Jacobs, Herbert, with Catherine Jacobs. *Building with Frank Lloyd Wright: An Illustrated Memoir.* San Francisco: Chronicle Books, 1978.

Kaufmann, Edgar, Jr. *Fallingwater: A Frank Lloyd Wright Country House.* New York: Abbeville Press, 1986.

Legler, Dixie. *Frank Lloyd Wright: The Western Work.* San Francisco: Chronicle Books, 1999.

Levine, Neil. *The Architecture of Frank Lloyd Wright.* Princeton: Princeton University Press, 1996.

Lind, Carla. *Wright at a Glance Series.* 12 vols. San Francisco: Pomegranate, 1994–96.

Maddex, Diane. *50 Favourite Designs.* London: Thames & Hudson, 1999.

_____. *Wright-Sized Houses.* London: Thames & Hudson, 2003.

McCarter, Robert. *Frank Lloyd Wright.* London: Phaidon Press, 1997.

Manson, Grant Carpenter. *Frank Lloyd Wright to 1910: The First Golden Age.* New York: Van Nostrand Reinhold, 1958.

Pfeiffer, Bruce Brooks, with David Larkin. *Frank Lloyd Wright: Master Builder.* London: Thames & Hudson, 1997.

Riley, Terence, ed., with Peter Reed. *Frank Lloyd Wright: Architect.* New York: Museum of Modern Art, 1994.

Sanderson, Arlene, ed. *Wright Sites: A Guide to Frank Lloyd Wright Public Places.* Rev. ed. New York: Princeton Architectural Press, 2001.

Secrest, Meryle. *Frank Lloyd Wright.* New York: Knopf, 1992.

Sergeant, John. *Frank Lloyd Wright's Usonian Houses.* New York: Whitney Library of Design, 1976.

Storrer, William Allin. *Frank Lloyd Wright Companion.* Chicago: University of Chicago Press, 1993.

Weil, Zarine, ed. *Building a Legacy: The Restoration of Frank Lloyd Wright's Oak Park Home and Studio.* San Francisco: Pomegranate, 2001.

Wright, Frank Lloyd. *Frank Lloyd Wright: Collected Writings.* 5 vols. Edited by Bruce Brooks Pfeiffer. New York: Rizzoli, 1992–95.

Wright reads in his office at Taliesin, surrounded by chairs like those he designed for the Friedman house (1956), Bannockburn, Illinois. At left is a floor version of his distinctive Taliesin lamp.
[© Frank Lloyd Wright Foundation]

INDEX

*Page numbers in italics refer
to illustrations.*

ACKNOWLEDGMENTS

It is obvious that a book of this nature could not have been completed without the generous hospitality of the homeowners. While skilled architects have created these magical spaces—and to them I am certainly indebted—it is the owners who care for the houses and make them shine. Most of the houses included are, after all, private homes, where people eat breakfast in their pajamas and argue with their spouses. I sincerely appreciate this opportunity to step into their private lives through this "biblio-visit." Most of us must limit our quest to experience Wright interiors to visits to the numerous public buildings scattered throughout the country. They continue to survive because of the generosity and efforts of corporations, government agencies, preservation organizations, foundations, and individuals like yourself. Therefore, to all of the owners and supporters of Wright preservation projects, thank you.

The near century of scholarship on the contributions of Frank Lloyd Wright was another vital component of this inside look at Wright's houses. Special thanks are extended particularly to H. Allen Brooks, Jeffrey Chusid, Donald Hallmark, David Hanks, Donald Hoffmann, Donald Johnson, Grant Carpenter Manson, Bruce Brooks Pfeiffer, Jack Quinan, Arlene Sanderson, John Sergeant, and posthumously to Henry-Russell Hitchcock and Edgar Kaufmann Jr. Meg Klinkow of the Frank Lloyd Wright Home and Studio Foundation Research Center, John Geiger and Louis Weihle of the Taliesin Apprentices Association, and Oscar Munoz at the Taliesin Archives also provided valuable information.

For special help with photographs, thanks are due to Melanie Birk and the Frank Lloyd Wright Home and Studio Foundation, John Howe, Joan Lupton and Steelcase, Tony Puttnam, Mildred and Alvin Rosenbaum, and Hollis Weishar and Taliesin Architects.

Finally, I am genuinely appreciative of the Frank Lloyd Wright Building Conservancy and my family for giving me the time to write this book.

Carla Lind

ABOUT THE AUTHOR

After *The Wright Style*, Carla Lind went on to write a number of other books on Frank Lloyd Wright. These include *The Lost Buildings of Frank Lloyd Wright: Vanished Masterpieces* and a twelve-volume series of miniature books: *Frank Lloyd Wright's Life and Homes, First Houses, Prairie Houses, California Houses, Fallingwater, Usonian Houses, Public Buildings, Lost Buildings, Dining Rooms, Glass Designs, Fireplaces,* and *Furnishings*. She previously served as executive director of the Frank Lloyd Wright Building Conservancy and restoration director for Wright's May house in Grand Rapids, Michigan; this project for Steelcase Inc. won numerous awards, including the President's Award honoring the best privately funded restoration and an Honor Award from the American Institute of Architects. Before that Lind served as executive director of the Frank Lloyd Wright Home and Studio Foundation (now the Frank Lloyd Wright Preservation Trust) in Oak Park, Illinois, which administers Wright's first home and studio and his Robie house in Chicago. She has lectured widely on Wright's work and has served as a preservation consultant on Wright projects, including for the Wisconsin Governor's Commission on Taliesin. At the University of Minnesota, Lind majored in interior design with an emphasis on the history of architecture.

The text for *The Wright Style* was composed in Gill Sans, a typeface designed by Eric Gill in 1928 for the Monotype Corporation in England. Gill Sans was modeled after the London Transport type that Edward Johnston designed for the London Underground Railway in 1916. With its clear geometric construction, Johnston's type was much more legible than earlier sans-serif forms. The display typeface was created especially for *The Wright Style* by Robert L. Wiser of Archetype Press. Named Prairie, this design is based on hand lettering that appears throughout the early drawings of Frank Lloyd Wright, especially during the period in which he was creating his signature Prairie Style houses.